AGENT OF INFLUENCE

GROVER NORQUIST AND THE
ASSAULT ON THE RIGHT

CENTER FOR SECURITY POLICY PRESS

ARCHIVAL SERIES

Agent of Influence: Grover Norquist and the Assault on the Right
is published in the United States by the Center for Security Policy Press,
a division of the Center for Security Policy.

Third Edition | April 22, 2014

THE CENTER FOR SECURITY POLICY
1901 Pennsylvania Avenue, Suite 201
Washington, DC 20006
Phone: (202) 835-9077 | Email: info@securefreedom.org
For more information, please see securefreedom.org

CONTENTS

Foreword..5

Letter to Cleta Mitchell, February 11, 2014.........................8

Executive Summary 12

Statement of Facts 17

The Muslim Brotherhood And Its Mission—
Including In America...17

Abdurahman Alamoudi—Muslim Brotherhood
Operative And Terrorist 22

Khaled Saffuri—Alamoudi's Right-Hand Man 26

Grover Norquist—Enabler of Muslim Brotherhood
Influence Operations 28

Suhail Khan—Muslim Brotherhood Princeling
And Influence Operator 31

'Secret Evidence' 36

Muslim Brotherhood Influence Operations Post 9/11 43

Endnotes...49

Afterword..71

Appendix I: Letter from Cleta Mitchell, March 21, 2014.........75

Appendix II: Letter from former Attorney General Mukasey
in response to Cleta Mitchell, April 18, 2004...................... 77

FOREWORD

This monograph reproduces a letter sent on February 11, 2014 by ten influential national security practitioners led by former U.S. Attorney General Michael Mukasey and President Clinton's Director of Central Intelligence, R. James Woolsey, to Cleta Mitchell, Esq. The letter conveys a Statement of Facts, together with an executive summary, that contradict representations made on September 21, 2011 by Ms. Mitchell to the Board of Directors of the American Conservative Union (ACU), on which she serves.

This third edition of *Agent of Influence: Grover Norquist and the Assault on the Right*, also features an exchange of highly instructive letters that occurred in April 2014 between Ms. Mitchell and General Mukasey.

The Statement of Facts relates the evidence that supports charges I have made since I first became aware in 1999 of the true nature of the Islamic Free Market Institute (better known as the Islamic Institute or II), which was then operating out of the office of Grover Norquist's Americans for Tax Reform (ATR). At the time, my organization, the Center for Security Policy, had just begun a seven-year sublet from ATR, which included a shared conference space and copier room.

Shortly after we moved into those suites, a colleague asked if I knew that there was an Islamist front group on the other side of that Xerox room. I did not at the time. But over the next seven, biblically long years, I had ample opportunity to establish that the Islamic Institute was closely tied to the Muslim Brotherhood. It also became clear that, with considerable help from Grover Norquist, II and its associates were conducting successful influence operations against the conservative movement, the Republican Party and the George W. Bush team—starting with the 2000 presidential campaign and, subsequently, the Bush '43 administration.

In the intervening years, I have tried to warn those on the Right—and anyone else who would listen—about the seditious designs of the Muslim Brotherhood, its stealthy "civilization jihad" and the associated subversion aimed at our nation's civil society institutions and governing agencies. Important insights into this Islamist group and its goals are contained in the Brotherhood's strategic plan dated 1991 which was entitled, "An Explanatory Memorandum on the General Strategic Goal for the Group in North America."

This document was introduced into evidence in 2008 in *U.S. v. Holy Land Foundation et.al.*, the largest terrorism financing trial in our country's history. It makes clear that the Brothers are engaged in America in "a kind of grand jihad" whose goal is "eliminating and destroying Western civilization from within."

The Statement of Facts notes that the Brotherhood's modus operandi, as laid out in this strategic plan, involves advancing its stated goal by—among other things—penetrating and subverting U.S. organizations like the American Conservative Union and the movement it aspires to lead. The Statement of Facts also documents the wealth of information from credible government, media and other sources available to anyone interested in knowing the truth about the Norquist-Khan Islamist influence operation.

Regrettably, such warnings have been met by many of Washington D.C.'s prominent conservatives with what can be charitably described as willful blindness.

Worse yet, repeated efforts have been made to suppress this information and silence the messenger. The zenith of this campaign was the adoption in September 2011 by the ACU Board of a resolution in response to Cleta Mitchell's memorandum. The resolution denounced me and endorsed both Grover Norquist and an officer of the Islamic Institute and Bush '43 appointee, Suhail Khan: "This Board declares its complete confidence in the loyalty of Suhail Khan and Grover Norquist to the United States."

Thanks to the national security leaders who transmitted the Statement of Facts to Cleta Mitchell and the Board of the American Conservative Union, the extent to which that "complete confidence" has been misplaced and continues to pose a danger to the nation and the Right is now available for everyone to judge.

What is more, a remarkable letter dated April 11, 2014 from Ms. Mitchell to General Mukasey (published herein as Appendix I) confirms the gravity of the ACU Board's error. In it, the author of the September 21, 2011 memo to her colleagues on that board admits that, "I have absolutely no expertise or involvement in [the] field [of national security]." She adds elsewhere in the letter that she is "someone who has absolutely nothing to do with national security, in any way shape or form" and that "I know absolutely nothing about national security other than what I hear and read in the news."

Cleta Mitchell nonetheless proceeds to describe as "ridiculous" the concerns expressed by General Mukasey and his co-authors about the presence on the ACU Board of two individuals with ties to organizations and individuals that promote the Islamic supremacist doctrine of shariah and the jihad it commands. She asks, "Why, pray tell, do you CARE (sic) who serves on the ACU board of directors? Is that seriously a concern of yours or a threat to national security"?

In other words, by Cleta Mitchell's own admission, the ACU Board has relied upon someone with "absolutely no expertise" about national security to evaluate the facts concerning Grover Norquist and Suhail Khan's involvement in Islamist influence operations aimed at conservatives. Such a person would obviously be ill-equipped to perform "due diligence" in evaluating such issues as: the nature of the Muslim Brotherhood's "civilization jihad"; the subversive operations that type of jihad entails; the identity of those conducting such operations; and the value to Brotherhood operatives and their enablers of penetrating the leadership of the American Conservative Union.

Judge Mukasey's response of April 18, 2014 (published herein as Appendix II) underscores why those with concerns about—let alone expertise in—national security matters would want the ACU's penetration by Islamist influence operators to be far more competently addressed. He observes to Ms. Mitchell:

> I think that the infiltration of organizations by people committed to the destruction of this country, and their sympathizers, is a proper focus for someone concerned about national security, a subject about which you concede complete ignorance. If there are people who call themselves conservatives and profess concern with protecting this country and its values, but who associate with and support people who are trying to undermine everything this country stands for, I think it is perfectly proper to point that out.

The former Attorney General closes his letter to Cleta Mitchell with the following admonition: "I very much hope that the American Conservative Union will address, as you have not—either in your September 2011 memorandum to its board or your most recent letter to me—the evidence of such infiltration in its ranks."

Unfortunately, to date, the ACU Board of Directors has chosen to ignore the Mukasey, Woolsey, et.al. letter and its attachment. Should that board persist in doing so—especially in light of Cleta Mitchell's self-impeachment as an arbiter of its exposure to infiltration of concern to the national security—members and supporters of the American Conservative Union will be on notice: The organization will henceforth be knowingly complicit in, and enabling, an assault on the Right on behalf of the Muslim Brotherhood and other Islamists.

Frank J. Gaffney, Jr.
President and CEO
Center for Security Policy
April 22, 2014

LETTER TO CLETA MITCHELL

February 18, 2014—Washington, DC: In the wake of the ominous announcement last week by the State and Homeland Security Departments that they are no longer going to enforce statutory prohibitions on granting asylum to individuals who have provided "limited" material support to terrorists, two proponents of such policies have been called to account.

Anti-tax activist Grover Norquist and an individual with longstanding family and personal ties to the Muslim Brotherhood, Suhail Khan, are the subject of a letter to leaders of the American Conservative Union (ACU) signed by ten influential national security practitioners. The signers include: former U.S. Attorney General Michael Mukasey, former Clinton Director of Central Intelligence R. James Woolsey, former Congressman Allen West, former federal prosecutor Andrew C. McCarthy, former Deputy Under Secretary of Defense for Intelligence Lieutenant General William "Jerry" Boykin and former Pentagon Inspector General Joseph Schmitz.

The joint letter transmits a Statement of Facts that responds to, and challenges, representations made concerning Messrs. Norquist and Khan in an exculpatory memorandum to the ACU Board written in September 2011 by one of its members, attorney Cleta Mitchell. The ACU Board was moved on the basis of those representations to endorse Norquist and Khan, both of whom serve as members.

The Center for Security Policy facilitated the compilation of the forty-five pages listing eighty-seven rigorously documented facts and fifty-five endnotes. Its President, Frank J. Gaffney, Jr. was the subject of the Mitchell memo that claimed on the basis of "fairly substantial due diligence" to have found no basis for Mr. Gaffney's longstanding charges that both Messrs. Norquist and Khan have enabled Muslim Brotherhood influence operations directed at the conservative movement and Republican Party.

Upon the release of the letter to Ms. Mitchell and the rest of the ACU leadership, Mr. Gaffney observed: "The signers of this letter with its attached Statement of Facts have afforded the Board of the American Conservative Union, the conservative movement as a whole and the Republican Party of which they are important parts an opportunity to address afresh a problem many have chosen to ignore—and, thereby, allowed to continue. These accomplished national security practitioners have rendered yet another service to their country and the cause of liberty. It is deeply appreciated."

Source: http://tinyurl.com/k2u6bu9

February 11, 2014

Cleta Mitchell, Esq.
Foley and Lardner LLP
3000 K Street, N.W.
Suite 600
Washington, D.C. 20007

Dear Ms. Mitchell:

It has come to our attention that you sent a memorandum dated September 21, 2011 to the Board of Directors of the American Conservative Union on which you serve.[1] In it, you made certain representations concerning specific, serious charges by Frank J. Gaffney, Jr. concerning the conduct of Grover Norquist and Suhail Khan. These charges relate specifically to their ties to and activities in support of Islamists inside the United States, including the Muslim Brotherhood, its operatives, front groups and agendas.

The following were among your representations:

> Because of the serious nature of Mr. Gaffney's allegations against Suhail and in my role as a board member of and/or counsel to several leading conservative groups, I undertook to read all the materials that Mr. Gaffney furnished to me. I have also reviewed the videos, DVDs and power point presentation that Mr. Gaffney provided as "evidence" of Suhail's role(s) in these various Muslim extremist organizations referenced in Mr. Gaffney's materials. While there was substantial material regarding the activities of the various organizations, there was absolutely nothing contained in any of the materials that in any way linked Suhail (or Grover) to such organizations or their activities.

> I repeatedly asked Mr. Gaffney 'where is the evidence of any relationship between these organizations and Suhail Kahn?' He never provided a single fact or any documentation that would tie Suhail to any Muslim extremist organization. None.

> I have conducted fairly substantial due diligence on this matter. I have reviewed and studied absolutely everything that Mr. Gaffney has sent to me related to his allegations against Suhail, I have met and spoken with Mr. Gaffney several times, I have repeatedly asked him for the facts to demonstrate any link between Suhail and any extremist organization(s).... and have asked him pointedly, "if Suhail is an 'extremist,' how did he obtain a White House security clearance?" After spending substantial time and effort to review Mr. Gaffney's allegations, I have

---

[1] http://tinyurl.com/ppwy4z3

concluded that there are simply no facts to support or substantiate his allegations against Suhail.

With respect to Mr. Gaffney's allegations against Grover, those are purely and simply character assassination. I have reviewed every-thing that Mr. Gaffney has presented to substantiate his continuing venom against Grover—but it is apparent that there simply is no basis whatsoever for those attacks. If there were any such factual support, Mr. Gaffney would have produced it years ago. It doesn't exist.

In the immediate aftermath of the receipt of your letter and apparently on the basis of your representations that there was no factual basis for Mr. Gaffney's charges, the ACU Board adopted a resolution addressing the controversy. The resolution, apparently erroneously dated September 20, 2011, states that the Board had "careful-ly reviewed documentation submitted in support of those claims" and "found [Mr. Gaffney's] purported evidence unpersuasive and the claims false and unfounded."[2] It went on to say that the Board "declares its complete confidence in the loyalty of Suhail Khan and Grover Norquist to the United States and…that the ACU wel-comes their continued participation in the work of ACU and of the American con-servative movement and profoundly regrets and rejects as unwarranted the past and on-going attacks upon their patriotism and character."

Given that your representations appear to have induced the American Conserva-tive Union Board of Directors to act in a manner that associated it unequivocally with the conduct of Messrs. Norquist and Khan and materially harmed the reputa-tion of Mr. Gaffney, you are requested to address the accompanying statement of facts that: (a) support Mr. Gaffney's charges, (b) contradict your representations and (c) place the ACU Board in the position of endorsing conduct on the part of two of its members that is at odds with the stated mission of the American Conservative Union—namely, "harnessing the collective strength of conservative organizations fighting for Americans who are concerned with liberty, personal responsibility, tradi-tional values, and strong national defense."[3]

These facts were in the public domain when you wrote your memorandum to the ACU Board, informed Mr. Gaffney's research and findings and would have been readily established by proper due diligence.

[2] http://tinyurl.com/ppwy4z3
[3] http://tinyurl.com/km8uajv

Sincerely,

Hon. Michael B. Mukasey
81st Attorney General of the United States

Hon. Allen B. West
Lieutenant Colonel, U.S. Army (Ret.),
Former Member of Congress

Lt. Gen. William G. Boykin,
U.S. Army (Ret.)
Former Deputy Under Secretary of
Defense for Intelligence

Andrew C. McCarthy, Esq.
Former Chief Assistant U.S. Attorney

John Guandolo
Former Special Agent, FBI

Hon. R. James Woolsey
Former Director of Central Intelligence

Adm. James A. Lyons,
U.S. Navy (Ret.)
Former Commander-in-Chief,
U.S. Pacific Fleet

Hon. Joseph E. Schmitz
Former Inspector General,
Department of Defense

Amb. Henry F. Cooper
Former Ambassador, Defense & Space
Talks and former Director, Strategic
Defense Initiative Organization

Clare Lopez
Former Career CIA Officer

cc: Hon. Alberto P. Cardenas, Chairman of the Board, American Conservative Union (with documentation notebook); Members of the Board of Directors, American Conservative Union

EXECUTIVE SUMMARY

In Cleta Mitchell's September 21, 2011 memorandum to the Board of Directors of the American Conservative Union, several representations were made that are rebutted by the attached Statement of Facts. These facts were all publicly and readily available to anyone doing, as Ms. Mitchell told the Board she had done, "fairly substantial due diligence." And they informed the materials Center for Security Policy President Frank J. Gaffney, Jr. made available to her and others.

The following (in bold) are Ms. Mitchell's representations, together with the factual information documented by the cited entries from the Statement of Facts:

I.   **"There was absolutely nothing contained in any of the materials that in any way linked Suhail (or Grover) to such organizations or their activities."**

The Statement of Facts demonstrates that Suhail Khan and Grover Norquist have extensive ties to "various Muslim extremist organizations," individuals associated with them and their activities. These include: organizations established in federal court as prominent Muslim Brotherhood front organizations with ties to the designated terrorist organization, Hamas; two convicted terrorists, Abdurahman Alamoudi and Sami al-Arian; and efforts to deny prosecutors an important counterterrorism tool vilified by such groups and individuals as "secret evidence." [See Facts 12, 13, 14, 15, 16, 21, 22, 25, 26, 27, 28, 29, 30, 31, 35, 36, 37, 38, 39, 40, 41, 42, 43, 44, 45, 46, 47, 48, 50, 51, 52, 53, 54, 61, 62, 64, 65, 68, 74, 78, 79, 80, 81, and 82.]

II.   **"I repeatedly asked Mr. Gaffney 'Where is the evidence of any relationship between these organizations and Suhail Kahn?' He never provided a single fact or any documentation that would tie Suhail to any Muslim extremist organization. None."**

Suhail Khan's parents, Mahboob and Malika Khan, were founders of several organizations demonstrated in federal courts to be Muslim Brotherhood fronts and associated with its Palestinian terrorist franchise, Hamas. Suhail Khan has also been involved personally with such groups, appearing at their meetings before, during and after his time in the Bush administration.

In videotaped remarks at several of these meetings, Suhail Khan used standard Islamist rhetoric (e.g., "What our oppressors going to do with people like us? We love death more than they love life.") He also expressed appreciation to Abdurahman Alamoudi, whom he identified as one of those "who have been helping me keep going" and for being "very supportive of me." [See Facts 12, 13, 14, 15, 16, 21, 22, 25, 26, 27, 28, 29, 30, 31, 41, 42, 43, 44, 45, 46, 47, 48, 50, 51, 52, 53, 54, 61, 62, 64, 65, 78, 79, 80, 81, 82, 83, and 84.]

III. "I have repeatedly asked [Mr. Gaffney] for the facts to demonstrate any link between Suhail and any extremist organization(s)....and have asked him pointedly, "if Suhail is an 'extremist,' how did he obtain a White House security clearance?""

As a volunteer at the White House, even a full-time one, Suhail Khan is unlikely to have held a security clearance—a costly investment generally reserved for paid government and contractor employees. He was, however, cleared to work in the Executive Complex to perform outreach to the Muslim community, thanks to his ties to others who had done the same during the Bush 2000 campaign—notably, Grover Norquist and Khaled Saffuri.

Suhail Khan did receive a security clearance in connection with his political appointment to a position in the office of the Secretary of Transportation in the aftermath of 9/11. Reportedly, he was moved from the White House to Transportation in response to information that a mosque in Santa Clara, California founded by Mahboob Khan had hosted a fundraising visit by Osama bin Laden's deputy, Ayman al-Zawahiri.

It cannot be determined whether in this instance, Suhail Khan—an individual known to enjoy the strong support of the White House—was subjected to a thorough background check, or whether at the time his Muslim Brotherhood connections would have been deemed a disqualifier.

(What has come to light recently, though, is a finding by the federal government that, since 1996, a contractor named United States Investigative Services (USIS) engaged in what it called "flushing" and "dumping" over 650,000 background investigations. According to the *New York Times*, the Department of Justice described this practice in a court filing as "releasing investigations that had not been completed." [See Facts 71, including Endnote 45, and Fact 84, including Endnote 52.])

IV. "After spending substantial time and effort to review Mr. Gaffney's allegations, I have concluded that there are simply no facts to support or substantiate his allegations against Suhail."

Mr. Gaffney's "allegations" tying Suhail Khan to Muslim Brotherhood front organizations, their influence operators and agendas are borne out by his own words, by those of one of the most prominent of those operators and by the reporting of others. [See Facts 12, 13, 14, 15, 16, 21, 22, 25, 26, 27, 28, 29, 30, 31, 41, 42, 43, 44, 45, 46, 47, 48, 50, 51, 52, 53, 54, 61, 62, 64, 65, 78, 79, 80, 81, 82, 83, and 84.]

V.   "With respect to Mr. Gaffney's allegations against Grover, those are purely and simply character assassination. I have reviewed everything that Mr. Gaffney has presented to substantiate his continuing venom against Grover—but it is apparent that there simply is no basis whatsoever for those attacks. If there were any such factual support, Mr. Gaffney would have produced it years ago. It doesn't exist."

As the Statement of Facts makes clear, there is abundant evidence to support Mr. Gaffney's "allegations" associating Grover Norquist with: organizations known to be Muslim Brotherhood fronts and their leaders; convicted terrorists Abdurahman Alamoudi and Sami al-Arian; the Islamic Free Market Institute, which received seed money from Alamoudi and was run by his long-time deputy, Khaled Saffuri; the penetration of Islamists into the Bush 2000 campaign and subsequent administration, especially at the sensitive moment when U.S. post-9/11 policies were being formulated; and the al-Arian initiative to repeal the statute permitting prosecutors to employ "secret evidence." [See Facts 12, 13, 14, 15, 16, 21, 22, 25, 26, 27, 28, 29, 30, 31, 35, 36, 37, 38, 39, 40, 41, 42, 43, 44, 45, 46, 47, 48, 50, 51, 52, 53, 54, 61, 62, 64, 65, 68, 74, 78, 79, 80, 81, 82, 85, 86, and 87.]

Conclusions

The Statement of Facts establishes the following:

1. Islamist enemies of the United States, led by the Muslim Brotherhood, are engaged in a concerted effort to destroy this country and impose their supremacist doctrine of shariah worldwide.

2. The Muslim Brotherhood is using techniques it calls "civilization jihad" to "destroy Western civilization from within...by [our] hands."

3. Political influence operations are among such techniques and are being used against America's civil society institutions and government.

4. Muslim Brotherhood front groups and operatives have targeted, among others, the Republican Party and conservative movement.

5. Leaders of organizations identified by the federal government as Muslim Brotherhood fronts—and, in some cases, tied to terrorists—were involved in influence operations targeting the GOP and conservatives during the late 1990s and some or all of the decade that followed. Such leaders included, notably: Abdurahman Alamoudi, Sami al-Arian, Nihad Awad and Khaled Saffuri.

6. Over the past fifteen years, Grover Norquist has had personal, professional and/or organizational associations with each of these Muslim Brotherhood operatives.

7. Norquist's connections, organizations and personal efforts have enabled the influence operations of Islamists, including those of Iran.

8. Suhail Khan has life-long associations with Muslim Brotherhood organizations and operatives—through his family and in his own right.

9. Khan has serially lied about: demonstrable connections to Abdurahman Alamoudi; the nature of the Muslim Brotherhood front organizations his parents founded; his own ties to those organizations; and his work on behalf of the Muslim Brotherhood's agenda.

10. Representations that there is no factual basis for these conclusions are, themselves, without foundation.

STATEMENT OF FACTS

The following pages provide factual evidence concerning the influence operations and related activities inside America of Islamist enemies of the United States, including notably the Muslim Brotherhood. The facts cited have been assembled from information that was publicly available prior to the 21st of September 2011.[1]

That is the date of a memorandum by American Conservative Union (ACU) Board of Directors member Cleta Mitchell sent to other members of the board (http://tinyurl.com/pxspfwf). In this memo, written on her law firm's letterhead, the author declared that she had done "fairly substantial due diligence" concerning charges by Frank J. Gaffney, Jr. concerning the associations and activities of two other ACU board members, Grover Norquist and Suhail Khan and found, among other things, "I have concluded that there are simply no facts to support or substantiate his allegations against Suhail" and "it is apparent that there simply is no basis whatsoever for" Mr. Gaffney's charges against Grover Norquist.

This document offers a basis for evaluating Ms. Mitchell's conclusions.

THE MUSLIM BROTHERHOOD AND ITS MISSION—INCLUDING IN AMERICA[2]

Fact 1: In October 2010, nineteen national security and intelligence professionals and other experts—including President Clinton's Director of Central Intelligence R. James Woolsey, the former Director of the Defense Intelligence Agency, Lieutenant General Harry "Ed" Soyster, the former Deputy Under Secretary of Defense for Intelligence Lieutenant General William "Jerry" Boykin and former federal prosecutor Andrew McCarthy—described the nature of the threat America faces today. They concluded:

> The enemy adheres to an all-encompassing Islamic political-military-legal doctrine known as shariah. Shariah obliges them to engage in jihad to achieve the triumph of Islam worldwide through the establishment of a global Islamic State governed exclusively by shariah, under a restored caliphate.

* * *

Since 9/11, most in this country have come to appreciate that America is put at risk by violent jihadis who launch military assaults and plot destructive attacks against our friends and allies, our armed forces and our homeland. Far less recognizable, however, is the menace posed by jihadist enemies who operate by deceit and stealth from inside the gates. The latter threat is, arguably, a far more serious one to open, tolerant societies like ours.

* * *

While the terrorists can and will inflict great pain on the nation, the ultimate goal of shariah-adherent Islam cannot be achieved by these groups solely through acts of terrorism, without a more subtle, well-organized component operating in tandem with them.

That component takes the form of "civilization jihad." This form of warfare includes multi-layered cultural subversion, the co-opting of senior leaders, influence operations and propaganda and other means of insinuating shariah into Western societies. These are the sorts of techniques alluded to by Yusuf al-Qaradawi, the spiritual leader of the Muslim Brotherhood, when he told a Toledo, Ohio Muslim Arab Youth Association convention in 1995: "We will conquer Europe, we will conquer America! Not through the sword, but through dawah.[3]"

The prime practitioners of this stealthy form of jihad are the ostensibly "non-violent" Muslim Brothers and their front groups and affiliates.

Source: *Shariah: The Threat to America; An Exercise in Competitive Analysis, Report of Team B II*, pp. 13-25. (http://tinyurl.com/46rh9s5)

Fact 2: "The Muslim Brotherhood is an international fundamentalist Islamic organization founded in Egypt in 1928 and is committed to the globalization of Islam through social engineering and violent jihad (holy war)."[4]

Source: Indictment, United States v. Holy Land Foundation, July 26, 2004 (http://tinyurl.com/ndfrur5)

Fact 3: Since the time of Hassan al-Banna, the Muslim Brotherhood's credo has been: "Allah is our objective. The Quran is our constitution. The Prophet is our leader. Jihad is our way. And death for Allah is our most exalted wish."

Source: The Muslim Brotherhood's Fifth Supreme Guide, Mustafa Mashhur, *Jihad is the Way*, translated by Palestinian Media Watch, February 9, 2011 (http://tinyurl.com/8gp7mad, p. 7.)

Fact 4: Hamas is the Palestinian branch of the Muslim Brotherhood and a terrorist organization.

The Harakat al-Muqawamah al-Islamiyya is Arabic for "the Islamic Resistance Movement" and is known by the acronym Hamas. Hamas, which is sometimes known to its followers as 'The Movement' is a terrorist organization based in the West Bank and Gaza Strip. Hamas was founded in 1987 by Sheikh Ahmed Yassin as an outgrowth of the Muslim Brotherhood....Hamas' charter says that the purpose of Hamas is to establish an Islamic Palestinian state throughout Israel and by eliminating the State of Israel through violent jihad.[5]

Source: Indictment, *United States v. Holy Land Foundation*, July 26, 2004, pp. 1-2: (http://tinyurl.com/ndfrur5)

Fact 5: Hamas has been formally listed by the United States government as a terrorist group: "On January 25, 1995, Hamas was designated a Designated Terrorist Organization by the President in the Annex to Executive Order 12947. On August 29, 1995, former Hamas Political Bureau Chief and current Deputy Chief Mousa Abu Marzook was designated a Specially Designated Global Terrorist.[6]"

Source: Indictment, *United States v. Holy Land Foundation*, July 26, 2004, pp. 5 (http://tinyurl.com/ndfrur5)

Fact 6: A member of the Muslim Brotherhood Board of Directors for North America and senior Hamas leader, Mohamed Akram, wrote a strategic plan dated May 22, 1991 and entitled "An Explanatory Memorandum on the General Strategic Goal for the Group in North America" This document was meant for internal review only and was approved by the Brotherhood's Shura Council and Organizational Conference.

Source: "An Explanatory Memorandum on the General Strategic Goal for the Group in North America" Government Exhibit 003-0085 3:04-CR-240-G, *U.S. v Holy Land Foundation, et.al.* (http://tinyurl.com/cjagsed, Appendix II, pp. 285-296).

Fact 7: The Explanatory Memorandum was discovered by the FBI in August 2004 during the execution of a search warrant on the Annandale, Virginia home of Ismail Elbarasse who was wanted at the time on a material witness arrest warrant issued in Chicago for fundraising for Hamas. It was subsequently introduced into evidence in 2008 in the nation's largest terrorism financing trial, *U.S. v Holy Land Foundation, et.al.*

Source: *An Explanatory Memorandum from the Archives of the Muslim Brotherhood in America*, p. 5. (http://tinyurl.com/nqxy6qe)

Fact 8: The Explanatory Memorandum describes the "role of the Muslim Brotherhood in North America" as:

> The process of settlement is a "Civilization-Jihadist Process" with all the word means. The Ikhwan [the Muslim Brotherhood in Arabic] must understand that their work in America is a kind of grand jihad in eliminating and destroying the Western civilization from within and "sabotaging" its miserable house by their hands and the hands of the

believers so that it is eliminated and God's religion is made victorious over all other religions.

Without this level of understanding, we are not up to this challenge and have not prepared ourselves for Jihad yet. It is a Muslim's destiny to perform jihad and work wherever he is and wherever he lands until the final hour comes, and there is no escape from that destiny....

Source: *An Explanatory Memorandum from the Archives of the Muslim Brotherhood in America*, p. 5. (http://tinyurl.com/nqxy6qe)

Fact 9: The Explanatory Memorandum has as an attachment a list of twenty-nine groups under the heading "A list of our organizations and the organizations of our friends." The first three groups on this list are: the Islamic Society of North America (ISNA), the Muslim Students Association (MSA) and the Muslim Communities Association (MCA). Number 22 on the list was the Islamic Association of Palestine (IAP). A number of these organizations were listed as unindicted coconspirators by the Holy Land Foundation trial prosecution.

Source: Government Exhibit 003-0085 3:04-CR-240-G, *U.S. v Holy Land Foundation, et.al.* (http://tinyurl.com/cjagsed, pp. 295-296). Those individuals and groups identified by the *Holy Land* prosecution as Unindicted Co-Conspirators are listed (http://tinyurl.com/3uhx6lh).

Fact 10: Also introduced into evidence in the Holy Land Foundation trial were wiretaps of conversations leading up to and during a meeting in June 1993 in Philadelphia where members of the Islamic Association of Palestine, including Nihad Awad, met with Hamas leaders to found a new organization called the Council on American Islamic Relations (CAIR). According to this evidence, the purpose of the meeting—and for CAIR—was: "determining the strategies, policies, and frames of Islamic activism for Palestine in North America in the near and far stages in its following aspects: Political action and public relations. Popular action. Charitable action. Media action."

Source: "The 1993 Philadelphia Meeting: A Roadmap for Future Muslim Brotherhood Actions in the U.S." by NEFA Foundation Senior Analyst Josh Lefkowitz, November 15, 2007 (http://tinyurl.com/nphd5k5).

Fact 11: On September 11, 2004, the *Washington Post* published on its front page a lengthy investigative report into the Muslim Brotherhood and its operations, among other places, inside the United States. Highlights of its findings included the following:

Many Brotherhood leaders advocate patience in promoting their goals. In a 1995 speech to an Islamic conference in Ohio, a top Brotherhood official, Youssef Qaradawi, said victory will come through *dawah*—Islamic renewal and outreach—according to a transcript provided by the Investigative Project, a Washington terrorism research group. "Conquest through *dawah*, that is what we hope for," said Qaradawi, an influential Qatari imam who pens some of the religious edicts justifying Hamas suicide bombings against Israeli civilians. "We will conquer Europe, we will conquer America, not through the sword but through *dawah*," said the imam, who has condemned the Sept. 11 attacks but is now barred from the United States.

In his speech, Qaradawi said the *dawah* would work through Islamic groups set up by Brotherhood supporters in this country. He praised supporters who were jailed by Arab governments in 1950s and then came to the United States to "fight the seculars and the Westernized" by founding this country's leading Islamic groups.

He named the Muslim Students Association (MSA), which was founded in 1963. Twenty years later, the MSA—using $21 million raised in part from Qaradawi, banker Nada and the emir of Qatar—opened a headquarters complex built on former farmland in suburban Indianapolis. With 150 chapters, the MSA is one of the nation's largest college groups.

The MSA web site said the group's essential task "was always *dawah*." Nowadays, Muslim activists say, its members represent all schools of Islam and political leanings—many are moderates, while others express anti-U.S. views or support violence against Israelis.

Some of the same Brotherhood people who started the MSA also launched the North American Islamic Trust (NAIT) in 1971. The trust is a financing arm that holds title to hundreds of U.S. mosques and manages bank accounts for Muslim groups using Islamic principles.

In 1981, some of the same people launched the Islamic Society of North America (ISNA),[7] which was also cited in Qaradawi's speech. It is an umbrella organization for Islamic groups that holds annual conventions drawing more than 25,000 people....

Source: "In Search Of Friends Among The Foes: U.S. Hopes to Work With Diverse Group," by John Mintz and Douglas Farah, *The Washington Post*, September 11, 2004 (http://tinyurl.com/ofo3fed).

Fact 12: The *Washington Post* investigation went on to note that:

In addition to the first generation of groups aimed at consolidating the U.S. Islamic community, a second generation arose to wield political and business clout.

One such group was the American Muslim Council (AMC), launched in 1990 to urge Muslims to get involved in politics and other civic activities. One of its founders was Mahmoud Abu Saud, who 58 years before helped Banna expand the Brotherhood, and who later became a top financial adviser to governments from Morocco to Kuwait, according to documents provided by the SITE Institute, a Washington terrorism research group that has written reports critical of the Brotherhood. The AMC folded in 2003, and a more moderate group has assumed that name.

One leader of the former AMC was Abdurahman Alamoudi, who U.S. officials and Islamic activists say is a Brotherhood associate.

Source: "In Search Of Friends Among The Foes: U.S. Hopes to Work With Diverse Group," by John Mintz and Douglas Farah, *The Washington Post*, September 11, 2004 (http://tinyurl.com/ofo3fed).

ABDURAHMAN ALAMOUDI—MUSLIM BROTHERHOOD OPERATIVE AND TERRORIST

Fact 13: According to the Department of Justice, Abdurahman Alamoudi was the "founder and former executive director of the American Muslim Council (AMC), the founder of the American Muslim Foundation (AMF), and...an influential member of other Islamic political and charitable organizations."

Source: Department of Justice Press Release, "Abdurahman Alamoudi Sentenced to Jail in Terrorism Financing Case," October 15, 2004 (http://tinyurl.com/p6ju78d)

Fact 14: According to 2004 testimony before the Senate Judiciary Committee's Terrorism, Technology and Homeland Security Subcommittee, among the "other Islamic political and charitable organizations" in which Alamoudi was "an influential member" were the following:

> 1985-1990: Alamoudi was executive assistant to the president of the SAAR Foundation in Northern Virginia. Federal authorities suspect the Saudi-funded SAAR Foundation, now defunct, of financing international terrorism. SAAR is the acronym for Sulaiman Abdul Aziz al-Rajhi, a wealthy Saudi figure and reputed financer of terrorism. Victims of the 11 September 2001 attacks allege in court that "The SAAR Foundation and Network is a sophisticated arrangement of non-profit and for-profit organizations that serve as front-groups for fundamentalist Islamic terrorist organizations."

> 1990: Alamoudi founded the American Muslim Council (AMC) as a tax-exempt 501(c)(4) organization, based at 1212 New York Avenue NW in Washington. The AMC has been described as a de facto front of the Muslim Brotherhood. The AMC's affiliate, the American Muslim Foundation (AMF), is a 501(c)(3) group to which contributions are tax-deductible. SAAR family assets financed the building at 1212 New York Avenue NW.

1991: Alamoudi created the American Muslim Armed Forces and Veterans Affairs Council (AMAFVAC). Its purpose: to "certify Muslim chaplains hired by the military." Qaseem Uqdah, a former AMC official and ex-Marine gunnery sergeant, headed AMAFVAC.

1993: The Department of Defense certified AMAFVAC as one of two organizations to vet and endorse Muslim chaplains. The other was the Graduate School of Islamic and Social Sciences (GSISS).

Source: Testimony by J. Michael Waller before the Senate Judiciary Subcommittee on Terrorism, Technology and Homeland Security, October 14, 2004 (http://tinyurl.com/op4xdph).

Fact 15: In what could be a case study of the Muslim Brotherhood's "civilization jihad,"[8] Dr. Waller also advised the Senate Judiciary Committee:

The American Muslim Armed Forces and Veterans Affairs Council (AMAFVAC) accredits or endorses chaplains already trained under GSISS or other places, like schools in Syria. AMAFVAC operates under the umbrella of the American Muslim Foundation (AMF), led by Abdurahman Alamoudi....One can trace part of the military chaplain problem directly to its origin: A penetration of American political and military institutions by a member of the Muslim Brotherhood [Abdurahman Alamudi] who is a key figure in Wahhabi political warfare operations against the United States.

Source: Testimony by J. Michael Waller before the Senate Judiciary Subcommittee on Terrorism, Technology and Homeland Security, October 14, 2004 (http://tinyurl.com/op4xdph).

Fact 16: In 1996, well after Mousa Abu Marzook was designated a Global Terrorist, Abdurahman Alamoudi declared his support for the Hamas leader: "I am honored to be a member of the committee that is defending Mousa Abu Marzook in America....I have known Mousa Abu Marzook before and I really consider him to be from among the best people in the Islamic movement Hamas, eh...in the Palestinian movement in general, and I work together with him."

Source: From "a translation of a transcript of an Arabic language news program, which aired on the ANA network, dated March 22, 1996, in which Alamoudi was interviewed in response to accusations that he was a supporter of Hamas," cited in *United States vs. Abdurahman Muhammad Alamoudi*, Supplemental Declaration for Detention by Brett Gentrup, Special Agent, U.S. Immigration and Customs Enforcement Bureau, p. 12 (http://tinyurl.com/qanvj2t).

Fact 17: Alamoudi told the annual convention of the Islamic Association of Palestine in Illinois in December 1996: "It depends on me and you, either we do it now or we do it after a hundred years, but this country will become a Muslim country. And I [think] if we are outside this country we can say 'oh, Allah, destroy America,' but once we are here, our mission in this country is to change it."

Source: Audio recording of Alamoudi's remarks (http://tinyurl.com/q2z97pl).

Fact 18: On October 28, 2000, Alamoudi publicly declared in Washington's Lafayette Square: "I have been labeled by the media in New York to be a supporter of Hamas... Anybody support Hamas here? Hear that, Bill Clinton? We are all supporters of Hamas. I wish they added that I am also a supporter of Hezbollah... Does anybody support Hezbollah here? I want you to send a message. It's an occupation, stupid... Hamas is fighting an occupation. It's a legal fight."

Source: Video recording of Alamoudi's remarks (http://tinyurl.com/c767ob5). Transcript included in sworn complaint by Immigration and Customs Enforcement Special Agent Brett Gentrup, September 30, 2003 (http://tinyurl.com/njm9flv).

Fact 19: Alamoudi was photographed at a gathering of jihadists—including violent ones identified as terrorists or representatives of designated terrorist organizations—at the "First Conference on Jerusalem" held in Beirut, Lebanon on January 29, 2001. Shown standing beside him were three other American terrorists: Ahmed Yusef, Yaser Bushnaq, and Imad-ad-Dean Ahmad.[9]

Source: Photograph at the Minaret of Freedom Institute website (http://tinyurl.com/pmt4mv7).

Fact 20: Abdurahman Alamoudi signed the articles of incorporation for the Islamic Society of Boston mosque in Cambridge, listing himself as its president. The two alleged perpetrators of the April 15, 2013 Boston Marathon bombing worshiped there, as did a number of others with ties to jihadist terrorism.

Source: "Mosque That Boston Suspects Attended Has Radical Ties," *USA Today*, April 26, 2013 (http://tinyurl.com/nk5l8vx)

Fact 21: In September 2004, Alamoudi was indicted by a federal grand jury for, among other illegal activities, "falsely concealing his affiliation with Mousa Abu Marzook, who had been named a Specially Designated Terrorist under Executive Order 12947 on August 29, 1995."

Source: U.S. vs. Abdurahman Muhammad Alamoudi, Superseding Indictment, 2004, p. 10 (http://tinyurl.com/oo98yaw).

Fact 22: Alamoudi was also indicted for having failed to disclose in his naturalization application that,

> "he was or had been: a Director of Mercy International - U.S.A., Inc.[10]; a Director of United Association for Studies and Research, Inc.[11]; affiliated with the Marzook Legal Fund[12], a.k.a. the Marzook Family Fund; the President of American Task Force for Bosnia, Inc.[13]; a trustee of the Fiqh Council of North America[14]; a director of [National] Muslims for a Better America[15]; a director of the Council for the National Interest Foundation[16]; and, a member of the Eritrean Liberation Front/People's Liberation Force[17].[18]

Source: Discover the Networks, "Mercy International (MI)," (http://tinyurl.com/peu367n).

Fact 23: In October 2004, Alamoudi pled guilty to three felony counts and was sentenced to 23 years in federal prison. As the Department of Justice put it:

> Court documents filed in conjunction with [Alamoudi's guilty] plea agreement describe how, *from November 1995 to September 2003*, Alamoudi devised a scheme to obtain money from Libya and other sources overseas for transmission into the United States without attracting the attention of federal immigration, customs and law enforcement officials. Alamoudi admitted to participating in a comprehensive scheme to conceal prohibited financial transactions related to Libya, his travel to Libya, and financial transactions designed to evade currency reporting requirements, among other things. (Emphasis added.)

Source: Department of Justice Press Release, "Abdurahman Alamoudi Sentenced to Jail in Terrorism Financing Case," October 15, 2004 (http://tinyurl.com/p6ju78d).

Fact 24: Abdurahman Alamoudi's dealings with Libya were not restricted to illegal financial transactions and his efforts to conceal them from federal authorities. The October 2004 Department of Justice press release about his conviction declared:

> Alamoudi made at least 10 trips to Libya, many lasting as long as five days. According to court documents, while in Libya, Alamoudi participated in meetings with Libyan government officials. Initially, during a meeting on March 13, 2003, Alamoudi and Libyan government officials discussed creating "headaches" and disruptions in Saudi Arabia. As the scheme continued, however, Alamoudi learned that the actual objective was the assassination of Saudi Crown Prince Abdullah. Alamoudi participated in recruiting participants for this plot by introducing the Libyans to two Saudi dissidents in London and facilitating the transfer of hundreds of thousands of dollars of cash from the Libyans to those dissidents to finance the plot.

Source: Department of Justice Press Release, "Abdurahman Alamoudi Sentenced to Jail in Terrorism Financing Case," October 15, 2004 (http://tinyurl.com/p6ju78d).

Fact 25: The Treasury Department issued a press release on July 14, 2005 declaring:

> According to information available to the U.S. Government, the September 2003 arrest of Alamoudi was a severe blow to al Qaeda, as Alamoudi had a close relationship with al Qaeda and had raised money for al Qaeda in the United States.

Source: Department of the Treasury Press Release, "Treasury Designates Movement for Islamic Reform in Arabia (MIRA) for Support to Al Qaeda," (http://tinyurl.com/ol5f2zn).

Fact 26: Prior to his arrest and conviction, Alamoudi engaged in political influence operations. As *Insight* Magazine reported in 2003:

> Alamoudi ran, directed, founded or funded at least 15 Muslim political-action and charitable groups that have taken over the public voice of Islamic Americans. Through a mix of civil-rights complaints, Old Left-style political coalitions and sheer persistence, Alamoudi helped inch the image of U.S.-based Islamists toward the political mainstream and induced politicians to embrace his organizations.

Source: "The GOP's Grover Norquist Problem and the Republican Debate" by Michelle Malkin, January 5, 2009 (http://tinyurl.com/8v2dvr).

KHALED SAFFURI—ALAMOUDI'S RIGHT-HAND MAN

Fact 27: Abdurahman Alamoudi's director for government affairs at the American Muslim Council and executive director at the American Task Force for Bosnia was Khaled Saffuri.[19]

Source: Islamic Free Market Institute website at Archive.org (http://tinyurl.com/posbjan) and American Task Force for Bosnia 1997 IRS Form 990 (http://tinyurl.com/ot3kdd6).

Fact 28: Saffuri served as treasurer from 1993-1998 of the National Muslims for a Better America, a political action committee tied to the American Muslim Council.[20]

Source: Saffuri interview with Kenneth Timmerman recounted in "Islamists' Front Man," *Insight Magazine*, February 24, 2004 (http://tinyurl.com/njkkp8p) and NMBC's Federal Election Commission filings for 1993-1998.

Fact 29: According to *Unholy Terror: Bosnia, Al Qaeda and the Rise of Global Jihad* by John Schindler, the American Task Force for Bosnia was an al Qaeda front:

> Islamist radicals played an important role in Sarajevo's public relations campaign in America. The most important bin Laden front working Washington on the Party of Democratic Action (SDA)'s behalf was the American Task Force for Bosnia, a registered charity that lobbied Congress and the Clinton White House.
>
> This organization, considered by Americans to be a group of moderate Muslims whose sole interest was helping innocent Bosnians, was headed by Khaled Saffuri, a Palestinian immigrant who cultivated links across the American political spectrum and proved an effective advocate of the Muslim cause in Bosnia. Saffuri worked directly with the White House on Balkan issues.

The task force shared offices with the American Muslim Council, headed by Abdurahman Alamoudi, who was also the task force's treasurer. Saffuri made several suspicious month-long trips to Bosnia while Alamoudi was the deputy director of Taibah International Aid Association, which had offices in Bosnia and had been founded by Abdullah bin Laden, Osama's cousin.

Source: John Schindler, *Unholy Terror: Bosnia, Al Qaeda and the Rise of Global Jihad*, p. 122 (http://tinyurl.com/q58edtd).

Fact 30: In 1998, Khaled Saffuri, founded the Islamic Free Market Institute (IFMI, also known as the Islamic Institute). According to the *Wall Street Journal*, "To run the nonprofit's day-to-day operations, [Grover] Norquist turned to Khalid Saffuri, a Palestinian-American raised in Kuwait who had been an official of [Alamoudi's] American Muslim Council, a political group in Washington."

Sources: Islamic Free Market Institute website at Archive.org (http://tinyurl.com/posbjan) and "In Difficult Times, Muslims Count On Unlikely Advocate: Norquist, Famed Tax Foe, Offers Washington Access, Draws Flak," *Wall Street Journal*, June 11, 2003 (http://tinyurl.com/oewwess).

Fact 31: The Islamic Institute's web site featured a quote from the then-chairman of the Republican National Committee, Jim Nicholson: "The Institute's work in spreading the importance of conservative principles and the Republican Party in the Islamic community is compelling and important."

Source: Islamic Free Market Institute website, "About US: Making a Difference, Building Relationships" at Archive.org (http://tinyurl.com/nbcofov).

Fact 32: Khaled Saffuri coordinated Muslim outreach for the Bush 2000 campaign. One press account reported that Mr. Bush "even named Saffuri as the campaign's National Advisor on Arab and Muslim Affairs."

Sources: Islamic Free Market Press Release, "Wall Street Journal Highlights Growing Success, Influence of Islamic Free Market Institute: White House, Karl Rove Denounces (sic) Anti-Muslim Bigotry," June 11, 2003 (http://tinyurl.com/nbslmjg) and Franklin Foer, "Fevered Pitch: Grover Norquist's Strange Alliance with Radical Islam," *The New Republic*, November 12, 2001 (http://tinyurl.com/oebajak).

Fact 33: In May 2000, then-Texas Governor W. Bush met with Abdurahman Alamoudi and a number of other Islamists at his mansion in Austin. Among those present were Khaled Saffuri and Karl Rove.[21] According to *Insight Magazine*:

Alamoudi and other Muslim leaders met with Bush in Austin in July [2000], offering to support his bid for the White House in exchange for Bush's commitment to repeal certain antiterrorist laws.

That meeting, sources say, began a somewhat strained relationship between the self-appointed Muslim leaders and the Bush team. Some senior Bush advisers voiced caution to Rove, who is said to have disregarded such concerns, seeing instead an opportunity to bring another ethnic and religious group into the GOP big tent. A photo of the Austin event shows Bush with Alamoudi standing over his left shoulder, flanked by the former head of the Pakistani Communist Party, several open supporters of the Hamas and Hezbollah terrorist groups and other individuals Insight is trying to identify.

Sources: Photograph of then-Governor Bush with Alamoudi and other Islamists (http://tinyurl.com/ogorpz6). *Insight Magazine* in "The GOP's Grover Norquist Problem and the Republican Debate" by Michelle Malkin, January 5, 2009 (http://tinyurl.com/8v2dvr). Also, "Friends in High Places: Sami Al-Arian isn't the only prominent Muslim leader who posed for chummy pictures with President Bush. Many conservative Republicans are uneasy at the way GOP power broker Grover Norquist curries support from the Muslim community" by Mary Jacoby, *St. Petersburg Times*, March 11, 2003 (http://tinyurl.com/nohsvmr).

Fact 34: In his book, *Infiltration: How Muslim Spies and Subversives Have Penetrated Washington*, investigative journalist Paul Sperry concluded that:

> In truth, the Palestinian-born Saffuri's main interest is in promoting Palestinian causes, not the GOP, says a Republican source who has had dealings with him. "Khaled clearly has a hidden agenda, of using the GOP to legitimate Islamist groups and place their agents inside the government, which happens to be controlled by Republicans, he says. "And Grover is their ticket into the White House."

Source: Paul Sperry, *Infiltration: How Muslim Spies and Subversives have Penetrated Washington*, p. 281 (http://tinyurl.com/qzz9r73)

GROVER NORQUIST—ENABLER OF MUSLIM BROTHERHOOD INFLUENCE OPERATIONS

Fact 35: Grover Norquist served on the founding Board of Directors of the Islamic Free Market Institute and reportedly as its chairman.

Source: Islamic Free Market Institute "Friday Brief": "Islamic Institute Participates in College National Republican Committee Convention," July 6, 2001, at Archive.org (http://tinyurl.com/orpvo72); and Foer, "Fevered Pitch," *The New Republic*, November 12, 2001 (http://tinyurl.com/oebajak).

Fact 36: Norquist was identified as the registered agent for the Islamic Free Market Institute Foundation when its registration papers were filed in the District of Columbia on July 23, 1998.[22]

Source: District of Columbia Online Organization Registration Form, File 982399, Initial date of registration July 23, 1998 (Current Status: Revoked) (http://tinyurl.com/qhescqh).

Fact 37: In the Spring of 1999, the Islamic Institute received two $10,000 contributions (one dated February 8th was marked as a "loan"; the second was dated April 4th) drawn on the personal bank account of Abdurahman Alamoudi.

Source: Photograph of the checks at http://tinyurl.com/p8au9tt.[23]

Fact 38: On August 24, 2000, a check was issued for the Islamic Institute in the amount of $10,000 drawn on the corporate account of the Safa Trust, Inc. The Safa Trust is, according to evidence introduced by federal prosecutors in the *U.S. v Holy Land Foundation, et.al.* trial, "a Safa Group corporation." The evidence described the Safa Group as "a complex coalition of overlapping companies in Northern Virginia controlled by individuals who have shown support for terrorists and or terrorist fronts."

Alamoudi served as Executive Assistant to the President of the SAAR Foundation, the predecessor of the Safa Group, from 1985-1990.[24]

Source: Photograph of the check (http://tinyurl.com/ov357sa);[25] testimony of J. Michael Waller before the Senate Judiciary Committee's Subcommittee on Terrorism, Technology and Homeland Security, October 14, 2003 (http://tinyurl.com/ouxvj6u); and *Holy Land* evidentiary submissions (http://tinyurl.com/orgrrh2).

Fact 39: In connection with the request for a search warrant for the March 20, 2002 Operation Green Quest raids, United States Customs Service Senior Special Agent David Kane swore an affidavit which declared, in part:

> I am investigating a criminal conspiracy to provide material support to terrorist organizations by a group of Middle Eastern nationals living in Northern Virginia. These individuals operate or have operated over 100 different organizations, on which they commonly serve as corporate officers.
>
> These organizations include charitable organizations, educational and cultural organizations, for-profit businesses and investment firms. For the purpose of this affidavit, this group of individuals and the organizations that they operate will be referred to as the "Safa Group"....I have seen evidence of the transfer of large amounts of funds from the Safa Group organizations directly to terrorist-front organizations since the early 1990's.[26]

Source: Affidavit of David Kane, Senior Special Agent with the United States Customs Service, in the matter of Searches Involving 555 Grove Street, Herndon, Virginia, and Related Locations. March 2002 (http://tinyurl.com/qdozmgl).

Fact 40: Franklin Foer published an article in the *New Republic* on November 1, 2001 entitled "Fevered Pitch: Grover Norquist's Strange Alliance with Radical Islam." Highlights included the following:

> Norquist is one of the undisputed masters of Republican coalition building.[27] And so it is no surprise that he has turned his attention to

America's fast-growing Muslim population, which by some accounts now stands at seven million strong.

* * *

In the last few years, Norquist has pursued a Republican-Muslim alliance with a two-track approach. With conservatives, he has emphasized that Muslims are a good demographic fit for the GOP: well-off and socially conservative. "American Muslims look like members of the Christian Coalition," he wrote in *The American Spectator* this summer.

To Muslims, he has promised a sympathetic hearing for their causes. He has pushed Republican leaders to support a prohibition on the government's use of "secret evidence" in the deportation of suspected terrorists—an issue that jibes with Norquist's own anti-government agenda.[28] [For more on this issue, see the section entitled "Secret Evidence" below.]

And he has intimated that Muslim support for Republicans could change U.S. policy toward the Middle East. Appearing on a panel at a 1999 meeting of the American Muslim Alliance, alongside activists who complained about the "Zionist lobby" and Jewish "monopolizing" of Jerusalem, Norquist announced that "[t]oo many American politicians have been able to take their shots at Muslims and at Muslims countries."

* * *

Norquist helped orchestrate various post-September 11 events that brought together Muslim leaders and administration officials. "He worked with Muslim leaders to engineer [Bush]'s prominent visit to the Mosque," says the Arab-American pollster John Zogby, referring to the president's September 17 trip to the Islamic Center of Washington. Says Zogby, who counts Norquist among his clients, "Absolutely, he's central to the White House outreach."

Norquist denies being involved in "micromanaging the specifics" of White House meetings, but admits "I have been a long time advocate of outreach to the Muslim community." In fact, the record suggests that he has spent quite a lot of time promoting people openly sympathetic to Islamist terrorists. And it's starting to cause him problems. [Paul] Weyrich, echoing other movement conservatives, says he is "not pleased" with Norquist's activity. According to one intelligence official who recently left the government, a number of counterterrorism agents at the FBI and CIA are "pissed as hell about the situation [in the White House] and pissed as hell about Grover." They should be. While nobody suggests that Norquist himself is soft on terrorism, his lobbying has helped provide radical Islamic groups—and their causes—a degree of legitimacy and access they assuredly do not deserve.

Source: "Fevered Pitch: Grover Norquist's Strange Alliance with Radical Islam" by Franklin Foer, *The New Republic*, November 1, 2001 (http://tinyurl.com/oebajak).

SUHAIL KHAN—MUSLIM BROTHERHOOD PRINCELING AND INFLUENCE OPERATOR

Fact 41: Suhail Khan is the son of Mahboob and Malika Khan, Muslim immigrants from Pakistan and founders of numerous Muslim organizations in the United States.

Source: Obituary ("Bio") for Dr. Mahboob Khan posted by [the Islamic Society of North America] (http://tinyurl.com/o2fq45x).

Fact 42: Three of the most important of these organizations—the Islamic Society of North America, the Muslim Students' Association and Muslim Community Association—were the top three named by the Muslim Brotherhood in its list of "our organizations and organizations of our friends" in the "Explanatory Memorandum" introduced into evidence by federal prosecutors in the *U.S. v Holy Land Foundation, et.al.* trial in 2008.

Source: "An Explanatory Memorandum on the General Strategic Goal for the Group in North America," Government Exhibit 003-0085 3:04-CR-240-G, *U.S. v Holy Land Foundation, et.al.* (http://tinyurl.com/cjagsed) *Shariah: The Threat to America*, Appendix II, pp. 295-296.

Fact 43: Suhail Khan has publicly acknowledged his parents' leadership role in organizations that have been identified by the federal government as Muslim Brotherhood front groups. For example, in July 1999, he told a conference sponsored by the largest of such groups—the very first mentioned in the attachment to the Explanatory Memorandum, the Islamic Society of North America:

> It is a special honor for me to be here before you today because I am always reminded of the legacy of my father, Dr. Mahboob Khan, an early founder of the Muslim Students Association in the mid-60s and an active member of the organization through its growth and development in the Islamic Society of North America.

Source: Video of Suhail Khan at 1999 ISNA Conference (http://tinyurl.com/qa4oshv). Cited quote at 1:50.

Fact 44: The memory of Mahboob Khan is held in such high regard by his successors at ISNA that they give an annual service award in his name.

Source: ISNA website description of the Mahboob Khan Muslim Community Service Recognition Award (http://tinyurl.com/ofl8z5h).

Fact 45: One of the organizations Mahboob Khan founded in Southern California is the Islamic Society of Orange County (ISOC). It hosted a visit in December 1992 by Sheikh Omar Abdel Rahman, better known as "the Blind Sheikh."[29] Rahman's visit preceded by two months the first attack on the World Trade Center, which he was subsequently convicted of masterminding.

A videotape recording of Rahman's remarks on the occasion reveals that he "dismissed nonviolent definitions of jihad as weak. He stressed that a number of unspecified enemies had 'united themselves against Muslims' and that fighting them was obligatory. 'If you are not going to the jihad, then you are neglecting the rules of Allah.'" The translator was ISOC's imam, Muzammil Siddiqi.

Source: "Azzam the American: The Making of an Al Qaeda Homegrown," by Raffi Khatchadourian, *The New Yorker*, January 22, 2007, p.57 (http://tinyurl.com/ypel4n).

Fact 46: Less than two weeks after 9/11, CBS reported that, "CBS News has learned [Ayman] al-Zawahiri, under an assumed name, visited the United States at least twice in the last decade on fund-raising tours of California mosques." The *San Francisco Chronicle* added on October 11, 2001 that two self-professed members of a terrorist cell recounted how, in 1995, "They brought Osama bin Laden's top aide to the Bay Area several years ago to raise money for terror attacks." Highlights of the *Chronicle's* report included:

> Experts said the existence of the Santa Clara terrorist cell—and its role in bringing al-Zawahiri here—showed both the boldness of America's terrorist enemy and the nation's vulnerability to infiltration by terrorist groups.
>
> "The very fact that someone like Zawahiri came to the U.S., that in itself should be quite stunning to many Americans," said Khalid Duran of Washington, D.C., a terrorism expert and author who has written about the Santa Clara cell.
>
> "He is the No. 2 man, bin Laden's right-hand man, and in a way even more. He is like his teacher, his mentor." In addition to fund raising, al-Zawahiri was in the United States "to see whom he could recruit here, what could be done here."
>
> * * *
>
> According to accounts of the confession [by the two terrorists, Ali Mohamed...and Khalid Abu-al-Dahab, who attended Santa Clara's an-Noor mosque"], Dahab said that in 1995, he and Mohamed had brought al-Zawahiri into the United States. The terrorist leader traveled under the alias of Abd-al-Mu'izz, using a forged passport that Mohamed had obtained.

Dahab and Mohamed introduced al-Mu'izz to leaders of the An-Noor mosque in Santa Clara.

Source: "Money Trail of Terror" CBS News, September 24, 2001 (http://tinyurl.com/ntxqrgj) and "Top Bin Laden Aide Toured State: Al-Zawahiri Solicited Funds Under the Guise of Refugee Relief," *San Francisco Chronicle*, October 11, 2001 (http://tinyurl.com/oggavjo).

Fact 47: Suhail Khan publicly declared his mother's role, as well as his father's, in founding the following groups—which have been identified as Muslim Brotherhood fronts, including in most cases by the Brotherhood itself in its Explanatory Memorandum:

> [My mother] worked hard with her husband to establish the Muslim Students Association, the Islamic Society of North America, the Council on American Islamic Relations, American Muslims for Global Peace and Justice...an Islamic center in Orange County and...an Islamic center and the Muslim Community Association in Santa Clara.

Source: Video of Suhail Khan speaking at the Islamic Society of North America annual conference in September 2011 (http://tinyurl.com/nnjalue). Cited comments begin at 8:57.

Fact 48: Suhail Khan's mother not only, as he put it, "worked hard with her husband to establish...the Council on American Islamic Relations." Malika Khan also served as an Executive Committee Member of CAIR's California chapter—a fact Suhail Khan acknowledged in a debate with David Horowitz on Sean Hannity's radio program on February 14, 2011: "My mother is on the California board of CAIR."

Source: CAIR California web site, June 2010, at Archive.org (http://tinyurl.com/oypur6r); and David Horowitz Debate with Suhail Khan on the Sean Hannity Radio Show, February 14, 2011 (http://tinyurl.com/ox5t4ex).

Fact 49: Suhail Khan sought to distance himself from CAIR during the February 14, 2011 debate with David Horowitz on Sean Hannity's radio program. Although he acknowledged that, "I've been to CAIR events" and "I know some of the individuals," he insisted,

> I've never been a member of CAIR. I have lots of problems with CAIR... and the people who have been associated with CAIR that have made comments, you know, in support of extremism, I definitely condemn all of that.... I'm not a supporter of CAIR. If CAIR is in any way associated with Hamas, I would support—be the first to support them being shut down.[30]

Source: David Horowitz Debate with Suhail Khan on the Sean Hannity Radio Show, February 14, 2011 (http://tinyurl.com/ox5t4ex).

Fact 50: At an American Muslim Council event in June 2001 (nine months after Alamoudi's declaration of his support for two designated terrorist groups, Hamas and Hezbollah), Abdurahman Alamoudi personally gave an award to Suhail Khan. In his introduction, he described Mahboob Khan as,

> a dear, dear brother who was a pioneer of Islam work himself. Many of you know [Suhail's] late father who was part of all kinds of work and... Suhail inherited from his father not only being a Muslim and a Muslim activist, but also being a Muslim political activist.

Source: Video of Alamoudi remarks at the June 2001 American Muslim Council convention in Washington (http://tinyurl.com/o9kpo7v). Cited remarks begin at 2:00.

Fact 51: Alamoudi also described Suhail Khan as "a dear brother," adding that he is:

> ...A pioneer, somebody who really started political activism in the Muslim community. And somebody different. A young man, not old and grumpy like many of us, but a young man who pioneered from many, many young men and women, who started political activism when it was a taboo for the Muslim community, no doubt about it.

> When Suhail Khan started not too many people were aware that we had to do something. I am really proud to be with Suhail Khan. Some of you saw him today in the White House but, inshallah, soon you will see him in better places in the White House. Inshallah. Maybe sometimes as vice-president soon, inshallah. Allahu akbar.

Source: Video of Alamoudi remarks at the June 2001 American Muslim Council convention in Washington (http://tinyurl.com/o9kpo7v). Cited remarks begin at 1:05. Transcript of relevant passage (http://tinyurl.com/484swlf).

Fact 52: Suhail Khan included Abdurahman Alamoudi among several individuals "who have been helping me keep going," expressing appreciation to Alamoudi for being "very supportive of me."

Source: Video of Khan remarks at the June 2001 American Muslim Council convention in Washington (http://tinyurl.com/o9kpo7v). Cited remarks begin at 5:05.

Fact 53: Among the reasons why Alamoudi would have been "very supportive" of Suhail Khan could be the jihadist sentiments the latter expressed at the ISNA conference in 1999. Particularly noteworthy are the following:

> Our freedoms, my dear brothers and sisters, are under attack....And these rights must be defended with all the determination, all the resources, all the unyielding vigilance of the believing mujahid.[31] That is the spirit of Islam. The mark of the Muslim.

* * *

This is our determination. This is the fierce determination we must re-
solve to bear in every facet of our lives. This is the mark of the Muslim.

The earliest defenders of Islam would defend [against] their more numerous and better equipped oppressors, because the early Muslims
loved death, dying for the sake of almighty Allah more than the oppressors of Muslims loved life. This must be the case where we—when
we are fighting life's other battles....

What our oppressors going to do with people like us?

* * *

I have pledged my life's work, inspired by my dear father's shining lega-
cy, and inspired further by my mother's loving protection and support
to work for the ummah [Arabic for the "Islamic nation"]. Join me in
this effort. Join hands with me in supporting the work of the many val-
uable organizations who have dedicated themselves to our protection,
to our empowerment as a Muslim ummah. Together, hand in hand, we
can work toward the cause of Muslim self-determination.[32]

Source: Video of Suhail Khan at 1999 ISNA Annual Convention (http://tinyurl.com/qa4oshv). Cited remarks begin at 6:40.

Fact 54: In his ISNA address, Suhail Khan exhorted the audience to maintain
Muslim solidarity in the face of harassment and worse from law enforcement and the
non-Muslim society.[33] Khan cited Islamic text: "A Muslim is a brother to a Muslim.
Neither he harms him nor does he hand him to another for harm." He went on to
urge his co-religionists to be "protectors of one another."

Source: Video of Suhail Khan at 1999 ISNA Annual Convention (http://tinyurl.com/qa4oshv). Cited remarks begin at 4:42.

Fact 55: In June 2001, in the presence of Abdurahman Alamoudi, Suhail Khan
described his father as "someone who dedicated his life to the community" and added
"I have always felt that I have to work in those same footsteps."

Source: Video of Khan remarks at the June 2001 American Muslim Council convention in Washington
(http://tinyurl.com/o9kpo7v). Cited remarks begin at 5:35.

Fact 56: Ex-Communist David Horowitz told the Conservative Political Action
Conference on February 12, 2011 that Suhail Khan's failure to disassociate himself
from his parents' movement is instructive:

> When an honest person has been a member of a destructive movement
> and leaves it, he will feel compelled to repudiate it publicly and to warn
> others of the dangers it poses. This is a sure test of whether someone
> has left the Muslim Brotherhood or not.[34]

I urge conservatives to school themselves in the nature of the Muslim Brotherhood and the networks it has spawned. And to be vigilant against its spread into the ranks of the conservative movement, the Republican Party and the government of the country we love.[35]

Source: Video and transcript of David Horowitz remarks at CPAC 2011 (http://tinyurl.com/n6s2wlk). Cited remarks begin at 11:15.

Fact 57: Three days after CPAC 2011 ended, David Horowitz, Suhail Khan, Cleta Mitchell and Frank Gaffney appeared together on Sean Hannity's nationally syndicated radio program on February 15, 2011. The host played clips from Khan's speech at the ISNA conference in 1999 and the American Muslim Council conference in June 2011. When Hannity asked Suhail Khan about his relationship to Alamoudi, Khan said: "I did not know Alamoudi. There is no connection there... there is no connection between me and Alamoudi. Period."

Source: Audio of the Sean Hannity Radio Show (http://tinyurl.com/p6cb52f). Cited remarks at 28:34.

Fact 58: On February 11, 2011, Suhail Khan told an audience on the margins of CPAC 2011, "There is no Muslim Brotherhood in the United States."[36]

Source: Florida Security Council video (http://tinyurl.com/pblh8ce). Cited remarks at 0:21.

Fact 59: On Sean Hannity's radio program on February 15, 2011, Khan denied that his father had any relationship with the Muslim Brotherhood. "There's no connection whatsoever to the Muslim Brotherhood—myself, my mother, my dad."

Source: Audio of the Sean Hannity Radio Show (http://tinyurl.com/p6cb52f). Cited remarks at 4:45.

Fact 60: On Hannity's show on February 15, 2011, Khan said, "[The Islamic Society of North America] is not a front for the Muslim Brotherhood."

Source: Audio of the Sean Hannity Radio Show (http://tinyurl.com/p6cb52f). Cited remarks at 6:19.

'SECRET EVIDENCE'

Fact 61: Suhail Khan worked in the late 1990s as Policy Director for then-Rep. Tom Campbell (R-CA). During that period, one of the Congressman's legislative priorities was the repeal of a statute known as "The Antiterrorism and Effective Death Penalty Act" (AEDPA, Public Law 104-132). AEDPA was signed into law in 1996 by President Bill Clinton and, as amended, allowed classified information to be used in deportation proceedings without being disclosed to the subject aliens.[37]

Source: Testimony of Rep. Tom Campbell before the House Judiciary Committee regarding "The Secret Evidence Repeal Act," May 23, 2000 (http://tinyurl.com/qcus6x6).

Fact 62: Preeminent among this statute's critics was Dr. Sami al-Arian, a professor of computer sciences at the University of South Florida, who paigned[38]against the use of what he called "secret evidence." Writing in *National Review*, Byron York described al-Arian and his interest and role in the campaign to repeal the AEDPA:

> In connection with the secret-evidence issue, Saffuri and Norquist made common cause with Sami al-Arian, the University of South Florida computer-science professor who had made a crusade of the issue. (Al-Arian's brother-in-law had been jailed and later deported in a terrorist investigation that made use of secret evidence.) Al-Arian headed the far-left activist group National Coalition to Protect Political Freedom, and made secret evidence its primary concern. Saffuri and Norquist shared a position with al-Arian's group on matters concerning secret evidence, and Bush was photographed with al-Arian during the campaign.
>
> Al-Arian also visited the White House in June 2001,[39] a year and a half before he was indicted on conspiracy charges as the alleged head of Palestinian Islamic Jihad in America. The indictment charged that al-Arian and his allies, "while concealing their association with the [Palestinian Islamic Jihad], would and did seek to obtain support from influential individuals, in the United States, under the guise of promoting and protecting Arab rights." During all this time, al-Arian's alleged terrorist ties were public knowledge, having been the subject of press reports and congressional testimony.
>
> * * *
>
> As with the Alamoudi connection, the al-Arian indictment left Saffuri distancing himself from a former associate. "If the charges are true, I feel deceived by him," Saffuri says. "But look, we didn't do work with Sami. He came by our office two or three times in the last four years." Norquist says he did not have a relationship with al-Arian....

Source: "Fight on the Right: Muslim Outreach and a Feud between Activists," by Byron York, *National Review Online*, March 19, 2003 (http://tinyurl.com/nvr4emj).

Fact 63: Four prominent civil rights organizations, led by the Anti-Defamation League, testified against the Secret Evidence Repeal Act (which they identified in a House Judiciary Committee hearing on May 23, 2000 as H.R. 2121) because, among other things:

H.R.2121 Could Force the Government to Release Terrorists Who Threaten National Security.

Because this legislation forces the government to choose between releasing a suspect or exposing intelligence sources, H.R. 2121 could lead to the release of individuals currently being detained who do, in fact, pose a terrorist threat. Law enforcement officials maintain that they cannot and will not expose sources and threaten the lives of personnel in order to move forward with a prosecution. Forcing this choice is tantamount to the ensuring the release of these suspects.

Source: Anti-Defamation League Statement on H.R. 2121—"The Secret Evidence Repeal Act" before the House Committee on the Judiciary, May 23, 2000 (http://tinyurl.com/qdzksmd).

Fact 64: Suhail Khan decried the use of secret evidence in his remarks to the Islamic Society of North America conference in September 1999:

Almost two-dozen Muslims are being held in federal prisons today, without federal charge, without bail and without the most Islamic and American opportunity to face their accuser and to challenge the evidence used by federal authorities to deprive them of their right to due process, their right to speech, association and their very right to freedom.

Source: Video of Suhail Khan at 1999 ISNA Annual Convention (http://tinyurl.com/qa4oshv). Cited remarks begin at 6:15.

Fact 65: While Suhail Khan was employed in the U.S. House of Representatives and working with his boss, Rep. Campbell, to repeal the 1996 counterterrorism statute, he became a member of the Board of Directors of the Islamic Free Market Institute. He also served as its chairman.

Source: Biographical information for Suhail Khan at C-SPAN's website (http://tinyurl.com/ounpyw5).

Fact 66: As a member of the Islamic Institute board and self-described "conservative activist" and "Republican,"[40] Suhail Khan was in a position to participate in, and benefit from, the access to the Bush 2000 campaign and its chief strategist, Karl Rove, that was enjoyed by the candidate's Muslim outreach coordinator—the Institute's Executive Director, Khaled Saffuri—and his sponsor, Grover Norquist. On August 23, 2010, in the midst of the controversy over the Ground Zero Mosque,[41] Khan wrote about what he calls "the work" the campaign engaged in to reach out to Muslims:

If Clinton was, as the author Toni Morrison once quipped, America's first black president, Bush was, at least momentarily, the country's first Muslim president. As early as 1999, he hosted a series of meetings between Muslim and Republican leaders, and paid a visit himself to an Islamic center in Michigan—the first and only major presidential candidate to do so. The 2000 Republican convention in Philadelphia was the first in either national party's history to include a Muslim prayer. On the campaign trail, Bush celebrated the faith of Americans who regularly attended a "church, synagogue, or mosque." After Muslim community leaders told him of their civil liberties concerns over a piece of 1996 immigration enforcement legislation signed into law by Clinton, Bush criticized it himself in one of his presidential debates against Vice President Al Gore.

The work paid off. By election day, Bush had been endorsed by eight major Muslim American organizations. He won more than 70 percent of the Muslim vote, including 46,200 ballots in Florida alone, prompting longtime conservative activist Grover Norquist—one of the few prominent movement figures to caution against the current wave of mosque demagoguery—to proclaim in the *American Spectator* that "Bush was elected President of the United States of America because of the Muslim vote."

Source: "America's First Muslim President: Muslim Americans Helped Elect George W. Bush, But Now They're Leaving the Republican Party in Droves. It Didn't Have to Be This Way," *Foreign Policy*, August 23, 2010 (http://tinyurl.com/psjgput).

Fact 67: An important part of "the work" that Suhail Khan applauded involved connecting George W. Bush with prominent figures in the Muslim-American "leadership." Notably, in March 2000, the campaign arranged for then-Governor George W. Bush to be photographed meeting with Sami al-Arian at Plant City, Florida.

Source: Photographs of Candidate Bush with al-Arian (http://tinyurl.com/qegtzod).[42]

Fact 68: With help from the Bush Muslim outreach team, Grover Norquist and Bush 2000 campaign senior advisor Karl Rove, Sami al-Arian secured a commitment from Candidate Bush during the second presidential debate with the Democratic contender, Vice President Al Gore, to "do something" about secret evidence were he to be elected.[43] Byron York detailed at *National Review* on March 19, 2003:

> Norquist reserved his highest praise for Saffuri's work in having "brought to the GOP's attention the most important issue for the Muslim community—the misuse of 'secret evidence' in immigration cases." Urged on by Norquist, Saffuri, and others, Candidate Bush denounced secret evidence during the 2000 campaign. In his second debate with Gore, he brought the subject up when asked a question about racial profiling: "There's other forms of racial profiling that goes on in America. Arab-Americans are racially profiled in what's called secret evidence. People are stopped, and we got to do something about that."

Source: "Fight on the Right: Muslim Outreach and a Feud between Activists," by Byron York, *National Review Online*, March 19, 2003 (http://tinyurl.com/nvr4emj).

Fact 69: The *Washington Post* reported on July 28, 2002:

> In Florida mosques and elsewhere, Sami [al-Arian] and his wife, Nahla[44], campaigned for Bush as the candidate most likely to end discrimination against Arab Americans. Sami Al-Arian says he delivered "considerably more votes" than the 537 that ultimately won Bush Florida and the White House. So, at [a June 20, 2001] White House briefing, the professor had earned a spot in the front row.

Source: "Talking Out of School: Was an Islamic Professor Exercising His Freedom or Promoting Terror?" by Richard Leiby, *Washington Post*, July 28, 2002 (http://tinyurl.com/q7a3v2t).

Fact 70: After the 2000 election, Norquist insisted that Muslim support delivered Florida to George W. Bush, and thereby secured for him the presidency. As Byron York reported in *National Review*:

> Citing surveys by Muslim groups, Norquist claimed that in the 2000 presidential election George W. Bush won more than 70 percent of the Muslim vote nationwide. In Florida, Norquist said, Muslims favored Bush over Al Gore by a 20 to 1 margin: "The margin of victory for Bush over Gore in the Muslim vote was 46,200, many times greater than his statewide margin of victory. The Muslim vote won Florida for Bush." (And, Norquist did not need to add, the presidency itself.)
>
> As impressive as that sounds, Norquist's numbers are open to serious question. Pollster John Zogby says there is not a great deal of information on Muslim voting, but "my data indicates that it was tilted Democratic in 2000. It went more for Gore and Nader than for Bush." Michael Barone, author of the authoritative *Almanac of American Politics*, argues that it is impossible to draw an accurate picture of Muslim voters, given the lack of exit-poll information. As for the claim that Muslims gave Bush his winning margin, Barone says simply, "Any 538 voters in Florida can claim credit for winning the presidency for Bush."

Source: "Fight on the Right: Muslim Outreach and a Feud between Activists," by Byron York, *National Review Online*, March 19, 2003 (http://tinyurl.com/nvr4emj).

Fact 71: According to Suhail Khan's biographical information, "After the 2000 elections, he aided the White House Office of Public Liaison in outreach efforts." In *Infiltration: How Muslim Spies and Subversives Have Penetrated America*, Paul Sperry wrote: "Norquist's group [the Islamic Institute] managed to place one of its staffers, Suhail Khan, inside the White House as the official gatekeeper for Muslims.[45]

Sources: Information about Suhail Khan disseminated in advance of the on-line poll that elected him to the Board of Directors of the American Conservative Union in 2007 at Archive.org (http://tinyurl.com/newc4k3); and Paul Sperry, *Infiltration: How Muslim Spies and Subversives have Penetrated Washington*, p. 281. (http://tinyurl.com/p73wfj7).

Fact 72: Evidence of Suhail Khan's involvement in Muslim outreach during his time with the Office of Public Liaison includes Abdurhaman Alamoudi's reference in his introduction to Khan at the American Muslim Council meeting in June 2001, that some in the audience had "visited Suhail Khan in the White House" earlier in the day. Khan subsequently told Sean Hannity that he was "sent" by the White House to the AMC event adding that "The White House would send me to eight, nine, ten events a day," suggesting that he was meeting with Muslim and other groups as a Muslim representative of the Office of Public Liaison with great regularity.

Source: Video of Suhail Khan at the 2011 American Muslim Council convention in Washington (http://tinyurl.com/o9kpo7v). Cited remarks begin at 1:40.

Fact 73: Suhail Khan found the White House a receptive place for the cause of repealing the secret evidence statute. In a debate with David Horowitz on Sean Hannity's radio program on February 14, 2011, Khan declared, "[Horowitz] says that I was carrying water on behalf of Sami Al-Arian at the White House on secret evidence. That was the president's policy. Not mine."[46]

Source: Audio of the Sean Hannity show on February 14, 2011 (http://tinyurl.com/ox5t4ex). Cited remarks begin at 7:57.

Fact 74: In July 2001, Grover Norquist received an award presented by Sami al-Arian on behalf of the National Coalition to Protect Political Freedoms, an organization made up of leftist organizations like the American Civil Liberties Union, the National Lawyers Guild and the Center for Constitutional Rights and Islamist groups like al-Arian's Tampa Bay Coalition for Justice and Peace and CAIR.[47]

Press accounts of this event include the following: "[In July 2001, the National Coalition to Protect Political Freedom—a civil liberties group headed by Al-Arian—gave Norquist an award for his work to abolish the use of secret intelligence evidence in terrorism cases, a position Bush had adopted in the 2000 campaign."

Norquist was credited with being a "champion of the abolishment movement against secret evidence." *Insight* investigative reporter Ken Timmerman says Norquist told the magazine he remains 'proud' of the award."

Sources: "Friends in High Places" by Mary Jacoby, *St. Petersburg Times*, March 11, 2003 (http://tinyurl.com/nohsvmr); "Media Ignores Grover Norquist's Islamist Ties And Activities," Militant Islam Monitor (http://tinyurl.com/crraeqr); and Michelle Malkin, "Alec Baldwin's New Best Friend is a GOP Strategist—No, Really!" Jewish World Review, October 22, 2003 (http://tinyurl.com/oxqkevp).

Fact 75: In remarks to the September 2001 Islamic Society of North America annual convention (immediately preceding those of Suhail Khan), Sami al-Arian described Mr. Bush's debate statement as "a promise"—one that had remained unfulfilled in the first eight months of the Bush presidency. He made clear that the candidate's commitment had been the basis for electoral support from him and other Muslims:

There has been a lot of talk about the endorsement of President Bush. We did not—the brothers did not endorse him because of Palestine or Iraq. There was a single issue. That was the issue of civil rights to us. There isn't any ethnic group in this United States that was empowered politically before they won their civil rights battles. Whether we like it or not, that civil rights battle has been defined to us in the issue of secret evidence. We wanted to raise that issue to the full front of the national debate....We're able to do that to the point that everybody heard it on national T.V. Millions of people heard what is happening to us.

So far the president did not deliver on his promise. We must hold him accountable. The jury's still out whether he would or wouldn't. And whether he would, that would depend on our involvement.

Source: Video of al-Arian's remarks at the Islamic Society of North America annual conference in September 2011 (http://tinyurl.com/nnjalue). Cited remarks begin at 0:40.

Fact 76: Al-Arian had a "plan of action" to demonstrate his allies' "involvement": He used an intervention at the 2001 ISNA conference to call on "everyone in the audience and everyone you know" promptly to inundate the White House with phone calls, e-mails and faxes supporting the Secret Evidence Repeal Act as a matter of "civil rights" for Muslims:

> Our hope is to generate thousands of calls to the White House asking them to support H.R. 1266. Secret Evidence Repeal Act. Again, that's H.R. 1266. The bill that has been sponsored, chiefly, by Congressman Bonior. That bill has to receive the support, has to receive the support of the White House so that eventually it will become the law of the land where no secret evidence will ever be used against anyone, Muslims or otherwise. [APPLAUSE] Brothers and sisters, the White House main number is 202-456-1111. Again, that's 202-456-1111. Every single person here, everyone you know, must call that number. Phone calls are the best, that's number one. I'll give you the e-mail later.

> You must call and say, please support the banning of secret evidence, please support HR 1266. We must get all Muslims, all our friends, all those who love the freedom and the freedom of association and everything that the Constitution stands for in the area of civil liberties and freedoms and due process. To make that one phone call, because then and only then we can say whether our involvement made a difference.

> The White House or the president's e-mail is *president@whitehouse.gov.*

> Secondly, please visit your congressman. Make a delegation to—make a point to visit your congressman and if they are not a co-sponsor yet on the bill, they must co-sign. You must make your voices heard.

Thirdly, please visit your editorial boards in the major newspaper in your town or city and let them know about this issue. Let them take a position in the editorial section as well as in the op-ed pieces.

Source: Video of al-Arian presentation to the ISNA annual conference in September 2011 (http://tinyurl.com/nnjalue). Cited remarks begin at 2:07.

Fact 77: In the wake of the ISNA conference and al-Arian's call for pressure on the President to fulfill his campaign "promise" to "do something" about secret evidence, a meeting on the subject with Mr. Bush was finally arranged with Muslim activists. It was to occur on September 11, 2001. Paul Sperry credits Suhail Khan with "arranging the ill-fated Islamist summit."

Source: Paul Sperry, *Infiltration: How Muslim Spies and Subversives have Penetrated Washington*, p. 281. (http://tinyurl.com/qzz9r73).

MUSLIM BROTHERHOOD INFLUENCE OPERATIONS POST 9/11

Fact 78: Due to the 9/11 attacks, the White House complex was closed. Grover Norquist and Suhail Khan escorted the would-be attendees of the secret evidence "summit" to a conference room on the second floor of 1901 L Street NW shared by Americans for Tax Reform, the Islamic Free Market Institute and the Center for Security Policy. The Center's president, Frank Gaffney, observed the group filing into the room, with Norquist and Khan being the last to join.

Source: Notarized affidavit by Frank Gaffney, September 28, 2013 (http://tinyurl.com/p953owa).

Fact 79: Dr. J. Michael Waller overheard part of the conversation that took place during the impromptu meeting in the second floor L Street conference room on September 11, 2001. He subsequently recounted that:

> It was in that conference room that Grover brought the Muslim Brotherhood folks to do, well, not to rally them to defend America against those who would destroy us, but contrarily to plot to put the Muslim Brotherhood front groups in the most positive light possible after 9-11—during 9-11 to make sure that the Muslim Brotherhood people would not be targets of any American opprobrium or official investigation.
>
> So it was damage control for the Muslim Brotherhood, not rallying American Muslims to come to the defense of America. That was the purpose of Grover's meeting that day on the afternoon of September 11th, 2001.

Now I know this personally in part because I spoke to some of the people involved. I knew and had been friends for years with some of the people who worked for Grover at Americans for Tax Reform. And were very upset as insiders about what they saw happening, but they couldn't say anything because their jobs depended on them going along with it.

But also during the meeting I was able to listen in to some of the discussion because my office, again, shared the same wall as Grover's Wednesday group conference room. So for the first time ever, I decided I'm going to hear what's going on there. Cause I used to attend the Wednesday group meetings.

And so I pushed up the ceiling tiles on my office and I was able to listen to what was going on next door. That's how I know it was a damage-control meeting and part of the discussion included how to condemn the 9-11 attacks and how not to condemn them.

And because some of the people present wanted to justify some of the attacks or refused to condemn the attack on the Pentagon because it was a, quote, military target, the general consensus was that they would condemn the attacks against innocent civilians with the implicit unstated understanding that this was not condemning the attack on the Pentagon.

Subsequently, there was a full-page ad that was taken out in the New York Times with similar language. Condemning the attacks on innocent civilians, but it was sort of the Muslim Brotherhood code word for we're not going to condemn the attack on the Pentagon. So that's what Grover Norquist was doing on September 11th, 2001.

Source: Video of remarks by Dr. J. Michael Waller (MuslimBrotherhoodinAmerica.com, Part 4, http://tinyurl.com/pthpynk). Cited remarks begin at 22:40.

Fact 80: In the days following 9/11, President Bush had a number of meetings and photo ops with Muslim Americans. With Suhail Khan "inside the White House as the official gatekeeper for Muslims,"[48] most, if not all, of his interlocutors were associated with Muslim Brotherhood front groups. Among those prominently featured at events held at the National Cathedral, the Islamic Society of Washington and the White House were: Khaled Saffuri of the Islamic Free Market Institute, Nihad Awad of the Council on American Islamic Relations[49] and Muzammil Siddiqi of the Islamic Society of Orange County and the Fiqh Council of North America.[50]

Source: Photographs of President Bush with Khaled Saffuri and Nihad Awad at the Islamic Society of Washington mosque (http://tinyurl.com/ofyhoed); and with Muzammil Sidiqqi at the White House (http://tinyurl.com/qax22pb).

Fact 81: On November 12, 2001, Franklin Foer reported on President Bush's meeting with Siddiqi and others at the White House:

On the afternoon of September 26, George W. Bush gathered 15 prominent Muslim- and Arab-Americans at the White House. With cameras rolling, the president proclaimed that "the teachings of Islam are teachings of peace and good." It was a critically important moment, a statement to the world that America's Muslim leaders unambiguously reject the terror committed in Islam's name.

Unfortunately, many of the leaders present hadn't unambiguously rejected it. To the president's left sat Dr. Yahya Basha, president of the American Muslim Council, an organization whose leaders have repeatedly called Hamas "freedom fighters." Also in attendance was Salam Al-Marayati, executive director of the Muslim Public Affairs Council, who on the afternoon of September 11 told a Los Angeles public radio audience that "we should put the State of Israel on the suspect list." And sitting right next to President Bush was Muzammil Siddiqi, president of the Islamic Society of North America, who last fall told a Washington crowd chanting pro-Hezbollah slogans, "America has to learn if you remain on the side of injustice, the wrath of God will come."[51]

Days later, after a conservative activist confronted Karl Rove with dossiers about some of Bush's new friends, Rove replied, according to the activist, "I wish I had known before the event took place."

Source: "Fevered Pitch: Grover Norquist's Strange Alliance with Radical Islam" by Franklin Foer, *The New Republic*, November 1, 2001 (http://tinyurl.com/oebajak).

Fact 82: Foer explained how such a meeting might have been arranged:

If the administration was caught unaware, it may be because they placed their trust in one of the right's most influential activists: Grover Norquist. As president of Americans for Tax Reform, Norquist is best known for his tireless crusades against big government. But one of Norquist's lesser-known projects over the last few years has been bringing American Muslims into the Republican Party. And, as he usually does, Norquist has succeeded. According to several sources, Norquist helped orchestrate various post-September 11 events that brought together Muslim leaders and administration officials. "He worked with Muslim leaders to engineer [Bush]'s prominent visit to the Mosque," says the Arab-American pollster John Zogby, referring to the president's September 17 trip to the Islamic Center of Washington. Says Zogby, who counts Norquist among his clients, "Absolutely, he's central to the White House outreach."

Indeed, when Jewish activists and terrorism experts complained about the Muslim invitees to Adam Goldman, who works in the White House public liaison's office, Goldman replied that Norquist had vouched for them. (Goldman denies this, but two separate sources say they heard him say it.)

"Just like [administration officials] ask my advice on inviting religious figures to the White House," says Paul Weyrich, another top conservative activist, "they rely on Grover's help [with Muslims]."

Source: "Fevered Pitch: Grover Norquist's Strange Alliance with Radical Islam" by Franklin Foer, *The New Republic*, November 1, 2001 (http://tinyurl.com/oebajak).

Fact 83: *Jerusalem Post* columnist Caroline Glick wrote on February 28, 2003 that "Khan was removed from his position after it was exposed that his father hosted an al-Qaeda leader during two separate trips to the U.S." Paul Sperry provided more details at *Front Page Magazine* on January 20, 2011:

The San Francisco Chronicle has reported that at least twice in the 1990s, [Suhail Khan's] father's mosque hosted Ayman al-Zawahiri, now al Qaeda's No. 2, and helped raise money for him—all while Mr. Khan's father was running the mosque as chairman of the board (as confirmed by the *San Jose Mercury News*). After the Chronicle and other major newspapers reported the Zawahiri fundraisers in 2001, Mr. Khan relocated from the White House to the Transportation Department.

Mr. Khan claims the reporting is false, but it's based on the court testimony of past members of the mosque, and the *Chronicle* has never issued a retraction.

Sources: "Politically Correct Terrorists," by Caroline Glick, Jerusalem Post, February 28, 2003 (http://tinyurl.com/llxnqej) and "Who Is Suhail Khan," by Paul Sperry, Front Page Magazine, January 20, 2011 (http://frontpagemag.com/2011/01/20/who-is-suhail-khan/).

Fact 84: Suhail Khan received a political appointment in the Department of Transportation working in the office of the Secretary, ultimately holding the post of Assistant to the Secretary for Policy. Khan says he underwent "a full and comprehensive background check and enjoyed a security clearance."[52] Given his position, he would have had access to information concerning such sensitive matters as: emergency planning; shipments by air, rail and sea of hazardous materials; movements of military personnel and equipment and nuclear weapons; TSA, port, rail and road security procedures; etc.

Sources: Suhail Khan American Conservative Union biography (http://conservative.org/suhail-khan) and Suhail Khan letter to the American Conservative Union Board of Directors, (http://suhailkhanexposed.com/2011/01/09/evidence-new-york-post-a-gop-moderate-muslim-or-not/].

Fact 85: When Grover Norquist was challenged over the role he and his Islamic Free Market Institute have played in promoting Muslim Brotherhood-tied individuals to the Bush campaign and administration—particularly in the days after 9/11 when the White House was most susceptible to their influence operations—he denounced his critics as "racists and bigots" and declared that "there is no place in the conservative movement"[53] for them. As Byron York reported in *National Review* on March 19, 2003:

> The conflict [between Grover Norquist and Frank Gaffney] began to emerge on January 31 [2003], at the annual Conservative Political Action Conference in Arlington, Va., when Gaffney participated in a panel discussion entitled "Safeguarding Civil Liberties in a Time of War." He discussed the threat posed by recruitment programs run by radical Wahhabi Islamists inside U.S. prisons, on military bases, and on college campuses. And there's more, Gaffney said: "I'm sorry to say there is an active and, to a considerable degree successful, [Wahhabi] political operation aimed not least at the Bush White House."
>
> Later, during a question period, Gaffney said he had recently received a press release from the American Muslim Council—which he called "one of the leading Wahhabist sympathizers, and, I believe, [Wahhabi-] funded organizations in this country"—announcing that a top AMC official had been invited to the White House. Gaffney continued: "And in this press release, they credited one Ali Tulbah [a Bush administration official] for having gotten them into the White House. It turns out that Ali Tulbah's father is one Hasan Tulbah, the treasurer of the Islamist Da'wah Center, a prominent Wahhabi mosque in Houston. But the reason he was able to influence whether [former AMC executive director] Eric Vickers and the AMC were present in this White House meeting was because he is also, I believe, the associate director for cabinet affairs in the Bush White House, responsible in his portfolio, if you can believe it, for the State Department, the Defense Department, and the Justice Department. This is not how we win the hearts and minds of peace-loving, pro-American Muslims. It is a perilous path, and I hope that it will be corrected."
>
> Gaffney's remarks were startling, not because he was wrong about Islamist recruitment efforts—he in fact appears to be right on target—but because he singled out Tulbah, and suggested that the low-level White House aide played a role in the Islamist political operation. In the weeks since, Gaffney has not offered any evidence to back up his charges. Instead, he now says the problem he was addressing was not Tulbah specifically, but the issue of poor political judgment at the White House. Nor have several experts on Islam and terrorism who are

generally allied with Gaffney been able to point to any problems with Tulbah.

Gaffney's remarks enraged Norquist, who responded in an open letter to conservative activists. "There is no place in the conservative movement for racial prejudice, religious bigotry or ethnic hatred," Norquist wrote. "We have come too far in the last 30 years in our efforts to broaden our coalition to allow anyone to smear an entire group of people... The conservative movement cannot be associated with racism or bigotry."

The reaction was explosive. Even if Gaffney had been wrong to mention Tulbah by name, some conservatives felt, Norquist's reaction was over the top. To make matters worse, Norquist used a standard rhetorical device of the Left: If you can't win an argument with a conservative, call him a racist. "I, for one, don't see it," says David Keene, head of the American Conservative Union and an organizer of the CPAC conference. "If you read the transcript [of the panel], you can see if Frank was right or wrong, but there was nothing racist or bigoted about it."

Source: "Fight on the Right: Muslim Outreach and a Feud between Activists," by Byron York, *National Review Online*, March 19, 2003 (http://tinyurl.com/nvr4emj).

Fact 86: The *Washington Times* reported on February 7, 2003 that "Influential national defense specialist Frank Gaffney and American Conservative Union President David A. Keene[54] yesterday separately accused Mr. Norquist of employing "Stalinist tactics" against those who disagree with Mr. Norquist's role in brokering access to the Bush White House.[55]

Source: The *Washington Times*, February 7, 2003 (http://tinyurl.com/nvc9qbs).

Fact 87: According to a front-page story in the *Wall Street Journal*, the late Paul Weyrich expressed concern about Grover Norquist's efforts on behalf of Islamist organizations and operatives:

Paul Weyrich, head of the Free Congress Foundation, a conservative Washington lobbying group, calls Mr. Norquist's dealings with Muslims "very dangerous." Mr. Weyrich adds, "We have to acknowledge we're at war and that it's very possible some of the Muslims want to establish a fifth column in this country."

Source: "In Difficult Times, Muslims Count on an Unlikely Advocate: Norquist, Famed Tax Foe, Offers Washington Access, Draws Flak," by Tom Hamburger and Glenn Simpson, *Wall Street Journal*, June 11, 2003 (http://tinyurl.com/oewwess).

ENDNOTES

[1] While the facts presented in the body of this Statement were all in the public domain prior to September 21, 2011, in the interest of completeness, several items (e.g., articles, a congressional floor statement, etc.) summarizing such facts that became available after that date are included in a few footnotes.

[2] For additional information on the history, goals, capabilities and infrastructure of the Muslim Brotherhood abroad and inside the United States, see "The Muslim Brotherhood in America" (www.MuslimBrotherhoodinAmerica.com), a free, 10-part online video course produced in 2012 by the Center for Security Policy.

[3] According to the IslamToday.com website, "The word 'Dawah' in Arabic simply means to invite to something (http://tinyurl.com/ntrmbgc). When it is used in conjunction with Islam it is understood to mean 'Inviting to the Way of submission and surrender to Allah.'"

[4] See also the Muslim Brotherhood's by-laws, Chapter II, Article 2, which declare the organization to be "an international Muslim body, which seeks to establish Allah's law in the land by achieving the spiritual goals of Islam and the true religion." The by-laws describe such goals as including: "The need to work on establishing the Islamic State, which seeks to effectively implement the provisions of Islam and its teachings." The by-laws also state that, "The Muslim Brotherhood in achieving these objectives depends on the following means: ...The Islamic nation must be fully prepared to fight the tyrants and the enemies of Allah as a prelude to establishing an Islamic state." (http://tinyurl.com/oljlwbc)

[5] See also a memorandum introduced into evidence in the Holy Land Foundation trial, "Islamic Action for Palestine: An Internal Memo," dated October 1992, p. 11: "With the increase of the Intifada and the advance of the Islamic action inside and outside Palestine, the Islamic Resistance Movement (Hamas), provided through its activities in resisting the Zionist occupation a lot of sacrifices from martyrs, detainees, wounded, injured, fugitives and deportees and it was able to prove that it is an original and an effective movement in leading the Palestinian people. This Movement—which was bred in the bosom of the mother movement, 'The Muslim Brotherhood'—restored hope and life to the Muslim nation and the notion that the flare of Jihad has not died out and that the

banner of Islamic Jihad is still raised." (Bates #ISE-SW 1B6410000377-0000383, http://tinyurl.com/ovp736c).

[6] CBS News reported on September 24, 2001: "The Islamic Association for Palestine and Holy Land [Foundation] were founded and funded by Mousa abu Marzook, a major investor in InfoCom. He's also the political leader of the terrorist group Hamas" (http://tinyurl.com/3uhx6lh).

[7] ISNA was listed by the Department of Justice as both an identified member of the Muslim Brotherhood and an unindicted co-conspirator in the *U.S. v Holy Land Foundation, et.al.* terror-funding trial (http://tinyurl.com/3uhx6lh). In addition, documents introduced into evidence in that trial in the Northern District of Texas revealed that ISNA is the "nucleus" for the Islamic Movement in North America, and is a Hamas financial support entity (http://tinyurl.com/oof5d3o).

[8] According to Dr. Waller's testimony, Alamoudi actually described his contribution to the civilization jihad on the occasion when, in August 1996, "the U.S. Armed Forces commissioned its second Muslim chaplain, Lieutenant JG Monje Malak Abd al-Muta Ali Noel, Jr. 'We have taken a long and patient process to bring this through,' Alamoudi said. He spoke of cultivating others to take posts in the political system and law enforcement: 'We have a few city council members. We are grooming our young people to be politicians. We also want them to be policemen and FBI agents.'" Testimony of J. Michael Waller before the Senate Judiciary Subcommittee on Terrorism, Technology and Homeland Security, October 14, 2004 (http://tinyurl.com/op4xdph).

[9] The HistoryCommons website posted a report (http://tinyurl.com/nlyz8jz) citing the *Jerusalem Post* and Fox News that described the other attendees and the conference this way:

> Participants include leaders of al-Qaeda, Hamas, Islamic Jihad, Hezbollah, and militants from Egypt, Pakistan, Jordan, Algeria, Sudan, Qatar, and Yemen. The conference is held with the purpose of uniting militant groups for holy war against Israel and the US. The participants create a new organization called "the Jerusalem Project," with the goal of winning total Muslim control over Jerusalem. The participants produced a document which calls for a boycott on U.S. and Israeli products and states, "The only decisive option to achieve this strategy [to regain Jerusalem] is the option of jihad [holy war] in all its forms and resistance... America today is a second Israel."

[10] As the David Horowitz Freedom Center's Discover the Networks resource notes, "Mercy International was named in a May 1991 Muslim Brotherhood document—titled 'An Explanatory Memorandum on the General Strategic Goal for the Group in North

America'—as one of the Brotherhood's 29 likeminded 'organizations of our friends' that shared the common goal of destroying the U.S. and turning it into a Muslim nation." Members of its senior leadership had close ties to Osama bin Laden (http://tinyurl.com/peu367n).

[11] Franklin Foer, "Fevered Pitch," *New Republic*, November 12, 2001: "In the 1990s, [the American Muslim Council] co-sponsored two conferences with the United Association for Studies and Research, which, according to the *New York Times*, a convicted Hamas operative named Mohammed Abdel-Hamid Salah in 1993 called 'the political command' of Hamas in the United States."

[12] "Muslims for a Better America, a self-described sister organization of the American Muslim Council joined with CAIR and the IAP to protest the court-ordered extradition [of Mousa Abu Marzook]. In a press statement released by the Marzook Legal Fund, the groups lamented "the concern that our judicial system has been kidnapped by Israeli interests." Excerpted from "Jihad In America" by Evan McCormick, FrontPage-Magazine.com, September 05, 2003 (http://tinyurl.com/2b9wo7e).

[13] See the Khaled Saffuri section below regarding the discussion of the American Task Force on Bosnia in *Unholy Terror: Bosnia, Al Qaeda and the Rise of Global Jihad* by John Schindler.

[14] According to the Global Muslim Brotherhood Daily Report:

> The Fiqh Council of North America (FCNA) is an organization comprised of Islamic scholars, most if not all of whom are associated with the Muslim Brotherhood global network, including Jamal Badawi who has been identified...as probably associated with the Shura Council of the North American Brotherhood. FCNA grew out of the activities of the Muslim Student Association (MSA) and later became affiliated with Islamic Society of North America (ISNA), itself an outgrowth of MSA.
>
> FCNA maintains a relationship with other similar bodies in the global Muslim Brotherhood including... the European Council for Fatwa and Research (ECFR) as well as the Islamic Fiqh Academy in Saudi Arabia. The ECFR, headed by global Muslim Brotherhood leader Youssef Qaradawi, is a component of the Federation of Islamic Organizations in Europe (FIOE), the Muslim Brotherhood umbrella group in Europe and its membership is also comprised of many individuals associated with the Muslim Brotherhood. Two individuals known to be ECFR members, Jamal Badawi and Solah Soltan, are also associated with the FCNA. (http://tinyurl.com/otozq4f)

[15] Investigative reporter Kenneth Timmerman scrutinized the Federal Elections Commission filings for the National Muslims for a Better America (NMBC) Political Action Committee (which—as will be discussed in the Statement of Fact's Khaled Saffuri section—was run for Alamoudi by Saffuri, his long-time deputy at the American Muslim Council).

[16] According to Wikipedia, the Council for the National Interest Foundation is "aligned" with the Council for the National Interest, an organization that has a record of promoting anti-Israel, pro-Arab positions and policies and had met with such organizations as the Council on American Islamic Relations and Hezbollah (http://tinyurl.com/3xy6u4).

[17] A profile of these Eritrean organizations is listed by the National Consortium for the Study of Terrorism and Responses to Terrorism, a "center of excellence" of the U.S. Department of Homeland Security and the University of Maryland. It indicates that the Eritrean Liberation Front and its successor, the Eritrean People's Liberation Front, were "nationalist" groups that "initially displayed characteristics of a Muslim movement and later flirted with Marxism" and were supported by Iraq and Syria (http://tinyurl.com/q3eg8ds).

[18] Alamoudi's failure to disclose these organizations allegedly violated, among other statutes, Title 18, United States Code, Section1001(a):

> ...Whoever, in any matter within the jurisdiction of the executive, legislative, or judicial branch of the Government of the United States, knowingly and willfully—(1) falsifies, conceals, or covers up by any trick, scheme, or device a material fact; (2) makes any materially false, fictitious, or fraudulent statement or representation; or (3) makes or uses any false writing or document knowing the same to contain any materially false, fictitious, or fraudulent statement or entry; shall be fined under this title, imprisoned not more than 5 years or, if the offense involves international or domestic terrorism (as defined in section 2331), imprisoned not more than 8 years, or both.

[19] Investigative reporter Kenneth Timmerman interviewed Khaled Saffuri for a report published in *FrontPage Magazine* on February 24, 2004 entitled, "Islamist Front Man" (http://tinyurl.com/njkkp8p). Among the questions Timmerman pursued was the nature of Saffuri's relationship with Abdurahman Alamoudi: "In his efforts to distance himself from Alamoudi, Saffuri claims he went to work for him at the American Muslim Council in 1995, but left some 18 months later after the two had a falling out. But documents uncovered during *Insight* [Magazine]'s investigation show that Saffuri had been working for Alamoudi since at least 1993 and stayed with him until May 1998."

[20] Kenneth Timmerman's investigative report revealed:

> While it was never a major lobbying force, NMBA is significant because its donor list includes a stunningly high proportion of individuals who have been publicly identified as leaders of terrorist groups, or have been arrested, expelled or currently are under investigation for allegedly raising funds for terrorist organizations.

Among the contributors to Saffuri's AMC-sponsored PAC:

* Hisham al-Talib, who lists his employer alternately as the SAAR Foundation and Marjac Investment Group, both controlled by Barzinji and raided by Greenquest on March 20, 2002.

* Muhammad Ashraf, "an officer and/or director of Safa Group companies including Sterling Investment Group, Sterling Charitable Gift Fund and York Foundation," according to the government's affidavit in support of the raid. Ashraf's residence at 12528 Rock Ridge Road in Herndon also was searched during the March 2002 raid.

* Mohammad Jaglit, a SAAR Foundation director considered by federal investigators to be a key figure in the terror-support networks. The affidavit cites Jaglit as "an active supporter of [Sami] al-Arian and [Palestinian Islamic Jihad], both ideologically and financially" and notes that letters accompanying checks he sent to al-Arian from the SAAR Foundation instructed al-Arian "not to disclose the contribution publicly or to the media." Jaglit's residence also was raided.

* Yaquib Mirza, a Pakistani national considered by authorities to be the financial wizard of the Safa/SAAR network, who appears as the accountant for scores of Barzinji companies.

* Basheer Nafi, identified in the affidavit as the "U.S. agent of PIJ [Palestinian Islamic Jihad]." Nafi, a 50-year-old Ph.D., was deported from the United States in 1996 for visa violations, according to government sources. According to a government indictment, he "was a member and founder of PIJ" while he was working with al-Arian and PIJ leader Ramadan Abdallah Shallah at the World Islamic Studies Enterprise (WISE) in Florida, now identified by federal prosecutors as a front for Palestinian Islamic Jihad.

* Iqbal Unus, a director of Safa Group companies "including Child Development Foundation," whose Herndon residence was raided.

Other donors to Saffuri's PAC whose houses or offices were raided by Green Quest, say federal authorities, include Wael al-Khairo, Ahmad al-Shaer, Ahmad Khatib and Ali Abuzakook—all Barzinji employees—as well as Mohammad Salim Attia, Hibba Abugideiri and Hussam Osman, who worked for the Saudi-funded International Institute of Islamic Thought, and Fakri Barzinji.

Timmerman also reported:

Altogether, say federal authorities, Saffuri raised slightly more than $28,000 for the AMC-sponsored PAC and distributed it to members of Congress including Rohrabacher and Democrats McKinney, David Bonior and John Conyers of Michigan, James Traficant of Ohio, Peter DeFazio of Oregon, and Nick Rahall of West Virginia.

What united all the recipients, who ranged from far-left Democrats to libertarians, was their support for Palestinian causes and their hostility to the state of Israel. (http://tinyurl.com/njkkp8p).

[21] In one photograph from the meeting Karl Rove is shown holding a copy of a book presumably presented to Governor Bush by the visiting Islamists, entitled *The Cultural Atlas of Islam* (http://tinyurl.com/ptbkwxn). It was co-authored in 1986 by a prominent figure in the Muslim Brotherhood's American infrastructure: Ismail Al Faruqi. Al Faruqi was the founder and president of the American Muslim Social Scientists (AMSS). According to the AMSS web site at Archive.org (http://tinyurl.com/o2s2hu5):

To appreciate the development and growth of AMSS, one needs to understand the evolution of the Muslim Students' Association (MSA) of the USA and Canada. During the 1960s, the first generation of Muslim students from abroad started to organize at various North American universities in order to maintain their knowledge and commitment to Islam. The major student organization that coordinated Muslim student activities among universities was the MSA, which was established January 1, 1963 at the University of Illinois in Champaign, Urbana. Due to its unique orientation and exemplary organizational structure, MSA served as an international role model for Muslim youth in the 60s and 70s and became the first Islamic foundation in North America to proactively introduce Islam to the larger North American society, while bringing Muslims in America a greater awareness of their Islamic identity.

This student movement helped institutionalize Islamic work in North America, as it led to the development of specialized Muslim institutions. The positive hands-on approach used by students to promote the study of Islam on campuses encouraged the establishment of AMSS in 1972 by such Muslim scholars as Dr. Ismail Raji al-Faruqi who served as its first president for three consecutive terms during his tenure as full professor of Islamic studies at Temple University in Philadelphia, PA. He co-founded AMSS with Dr. Abdulhamid AbuSulayman who was a PhD student at the University of Pennsylvania.

Global Muslim Brotherhood Daily Report describes AbuSulayman as "one of the most important figures in the history of the global Muslim Brotherhood." (http://tinyurl.com/pzzhf78).

[22] According to the *Weekly Standard*, there was no distinction between the Islamic Free Market Institute and the Foundation of the same name. The *Standard* reported about Norquist and the use to which he put the IFMI and a lobbying firm called Janus Merritt. Highlights included the following:

> ...In 1997, when Abramoff's longtime comrade Grover Norquist opened a lobbying firm of his own, he made Safavian a partner. The new company was called the Merritt Group, then renamed Janus-Merritt Strategies...

> Lassoing American Muslims into the Republican coalition has been a longstanding goal of Norquist's. To that end, he established the Islamic Institute in 1998. Officially titled the Islamic Free Market Institute Foundation, the group, according to its website, seeks to "create a better understanding between the American Muslim community and the political leadership" and "provide a platform to promote an Islamic perspective on domestic issues." The Institute also produces numerous pamphlets explaining how Islam is compatible with the free market. Norquist is chairman of the board. Safavian registered as a lobbyist for the institute shortly after it was born.

> A prominent American Muslim attorney, Khaled Saffuri, is the executive director of the Islamic Institute. Saffuri is also a friend of Abramoff's. His previous job was at the American Muslim Council, or AMC, an Islamic interest group with a controversial past. That past caught up with Safavian sometime in October 2000, when Janus-Merritt submitted forms to the Senate registering Omar Nashashibi—one of the firm's partners—and several others to lobby for Abdurahman Alamoudi, the then-head of the AMC. Safavian's name is also mentioned in the document.

> A naturalized U.S. citizen born in Eritrea, Alamoudi is now serving a 23-year term in federal prison for conspiring to assassinate then-Crown Prince Abdullah of Saudi Arabia. Put simply, Alamoudi is a radical Is-

lamist and terrorist sympathizer who openly supported Hamas and Hezbollah while a client of Janus-Merritt's. There's no way around it: The guy is a bad dude. (http://tinyurl.com/o5qm2p4)

Public records indicate that Norquist's Islamic Free Market Foundation sponsored $219,491 for twenty-one Members of Congress to participate in conferences held in the Middle East, principally Qatar (http://tinyurl.com/pzg6slq).

[23] Investigative journalist Mary Jacoby reported on March 11, 2003 in an article entitled "Friends in High Places" in the *St. Petersburg Times*: "Norquist and Saffuri founded the Islamic Institute in 1999 with seed money from Qatar, Kuwait and other Middle Eastern sources. Among the contributors, records show, was Saffuri's former boss, a Muslim charity director and founder of the American Muslim Council, Abdurahman Alamoudi. The records show Alamoudi gave at least $35,000 to the institute, although Alamoudi said in a written statement he did 'not recollect having been quite that generous'" (http://tinyurl.com/nohsvmr).

[24] Wikipedia cites two articles: "A Nation Challenged: U.S. Examines Donations of 2 Saudis to Determine if They Aided Terrorism, *New York Times* March 25, 2002, and "A Court Sheds New Light on Terror Probe, *New York Sun* March 24, 2008 in its listing concerning the SAAR Foundation, "The SAAR Foundation, which was dissolved in December 2000, achieved prominence as the key subject of a March 20, 2002 raid by federal agents, as a part of Operation Green Quest. The Foundation's overseas origins date to the 1970s. Its U.S. branch was incorporated as a 501(3)c on July 29, 1983 in Herndon, VA, and dissolved in December 2000, and renamed Safa Trust." (http://tinyurl.com/pswc425)

[25] Mary Jacoby's reporting indicated that the actual contributions from the Safa Trust were greater: "Also funding the [Islamic] institute were two Virginia-based nonprofit organizations. The Safa Trust donated at least $35,000, and the International Institute of Islamic Thought gave $11,000, the records show. Last March, federal authorities raided those groups and others in Operation Green Quest, a major assault on suspected terrorist financial networks." (http://tinyurl.com/nohsvmr)

[26] N.B. The linked source document is marked "Under Seal" and "(Proposed Redacted) Affidavit in Support of Application for Search Warrant (October 2003).

[27] According to documents in a federal law suit, Grover Norquist's coalition-building extended to helping Trita Parsi and the National Iranian American Council—which have been identified by Tehran's state-controlled media as part of the "Iran Lobby" in the United States—promote the mullahs' agenda. As reported by Clare Lopez and David

Reaboi in *American Thinker* ("Grover Norquist and the Iran Lobby," The American Thinker, November 14, 2011 (http://tinyurl.com/npmsc4q):

> ...The recent public release of emails exposed as evidence from an on-going 2009 libel lawsuit (595 F.Supp.2d 99 (2009), *Trita PARSI and National Iranian American Council, Plaintiffs, v. Seid Hassan Daioleslam, Defendant*). An email dated June 14, 2007 from Michael Ostrolenk, Co-founder/Director of [a Norquist-associated and -housed organization called the American Conservative Defense Alliance (ACDA)], to Babak Talebi and Trita Parsi of the National Iranian American Council among others, invited them all to a meeting at "our office," using the Americans for Tax Reform's Suite 200 [at 1901 L Street, N.W., Washington, D.C.] address in his email signature.
>
> There is also evidence that ACDA hosted at least one other meeting on January 21, 2009, while they were still based in the ATR Suite 200 at the L Street address. As exposed in the "Meeting Minutes" from the Parsi v. Diaoleslam evidence, ACDA hosted a meeting for the full CNAPI group. The minutes state that this meeting included a group decision, among "legislative goals for the 111th Congress," to "End the [U.S.-sponsored] democracy fund [aimed at promoting opposition elements favoring democratic change in Iran] as we know it."
>
> According to the Minutes, other goals for the so-called Coalition for a New American Policy on Iran (CNAPI) included such priorities of the Iranian regime as:
>
> (1) No new sanctions until diplomacy is underway; (2) Congress should establish benchmarks for Iran to meet, after which it will support rolling back existing sanctions; (3) End the democracy fund as we know it (with suggestions for an alternative); (4) Negotiate an incidents-at-sea agreement with Iran; and (5) Make it easier for humanitarian groups and charities to do business in Iran (reform Office of Foreign Assets Control procedures).

[28] It also "jibes" with the agenda of convicted terrorist Sami al-Arian, man who was subsequently determined by a federal judge to be a "leader" of, as well as fund-raiser for, Palestinian Islamic Jihad. As the Investigative Project on Terrorism recounted ("Al-Arian Resurfaces in New American Brotherhood Campaign" (http://tinyurl.com/oospbm6):

> "The evidence was clear in this case that you were a leader of the Palestinian Islamic Jihad," U.S. District Court Judge James Moody said during Al-Arian's sentencing. "You were on the board of directors and an officer, the secretary. Directors control the actions of an organization, even the PIJ; and you were an active leader."

Investigative reporter and author Paul Sperry wrote in *Infiltration: How Muslim Spies and Subversives Have Penetrated Washington*, p. 285 (http://tinyurl.com/nuxckad):

> Norquist has maintained that he has had very limited contact with al-Arian since he worked on Bush's campaign in Florida. In fact, al-Arian gave Norquist an award eleven days after his 2001 office visit [at Norquist's Americans for Tax Reform]. At a Capitol Hill ceremony on July 28, 2001, al-Arian's National Coalition to Protect Political Freedom honored Norquist as a "one of the champions of the abolishment movement against secret evidence."

[29] According to the *Los Angeles Times*, Rahman stayed "during his lecture tours of Orange County mosques" with two jihadists who attended the ISOC, Khalil Deek and Hisham Diab. They are said to have "influenced" another ISOC attendee: future al Qaeda propagandist, Adam Gadahn (a.k.a. "Azzam the American"). *Los Angeles Times*, "O.C. Man Rises in al Qaeda: 'Azzam the American,' or Adam Gadahn, Has Moved from Translator to Propagandist," October 8, 2006 (http://tinyurl.com/o9zmal4).

[30] Four federal judges have affirmed the federal government's contention that not only the Council on American Islamic Relations but other organizations founded by Suhail Khan's parents are "affiliated" with Hamas. For example, prosecutors successfully argued in district court in *U.S. v Holy Land Foundation, et.al.* and the Fifth Circuit which heard an appeal that, as District Court Judge Jorge Solis put it in a July 1, 2009 (ruling unsealed in November 2010): "The government has produced ample evidence to establish the associations of CAIR, ISNA, NAIT, with NAIT, the Islamic Association for Palestine, and with Hamas" (http://tinyurl.com/28rv3az).

[31] The Free Dictionary's entry for "Mujahideen" has it as the nominative plural of "Mujahid" (Arabic: مجاهد *muǧāhid*, oblique plural مجاهدون *muǧāhidūn*, nominative plural مجاهدين *muǧāhidīn* 'strugglers' or 'people doing jihad'). "Mujahideen—Muslim guerrilla warriors engaged in a jihad." Also, "Mujahid—a Muslim engaged in what he considers to be a jihad…. a military force of Muslim guerilla warriors engaged in a jihad." (http://tinyurl.com/o88bjhl) and (http://tinyurl.com/os2leh2).

[32] Such statements are not "cherry-picked" or quoted out of context in a misleading way from a speech Suhail Khan insists was about "civil rights." As David Horowitz observed on Sean Hannity's show on February 15, 2011 (http://tinyurl.com/pvt2lq6), while there are passages in Khan's 1999 ISNA speech that refer to prominent black Americans, "the speech is about the oppression, not about civil rights. He does mention Rosa Parks. But it's to appropriate the moral mantle of the civil rights movement for a cause which is to stop America from protecting itself against Muslim radicals."

[33] Discouraging Muslims from cooperating with the law enforcement community has been a hardy perennial among Muslim Brotherhood operatives, particularly since 9/11. As Frank Gaffney recounts in an article entitled "A Troubling Influence" published by *Front Page Magazine* on December 9, 2003 (http://tinyurl.com/29glebo):

> ...A few weeks after 9/11, I made an intervention [at Grover Norquist's Wednesday Group meeting of the so-called "Center-Right Coalition" to decry the fact that Alamoudi's American Muslim Council was among the groups invited to the White House. I observed that on the same day its representatives were meeting with the President and his senior subordinates to talk about how Muslims could help with the war on terror, the AMC's website featured a box headlined "Know Your Rights." A click on the proferred hyperlink took you to a joint statement urging Muslims not to talk to the FBI.

> The statement was issued in the name of an organization of which the AMC was a member: the National Coalition to Protect Political Freedom (NCPPF)—a virtual legal aid office for terrorists. At the time, a South Florida University professor named Sami al-Arian was the NCPPF's president. As will be discussed below, he was also Secretary of the worldwide governing council of a terrorist organization called Palestinian Islamic Jihad (PIJ), responsible for 99 suicide-bombing victims.

> I suggested to the Wednesday Group that the White House would surely have been astonished to discover that it was dignifying so-called Muslim leaders who were urging their co-religionists not to cooperate with law enforcement. I also pointedly observed—without mentioning names—that those responsible for facilitating the President's Muslim outreach, who profess to support him and wish him success, should take pains to avoid including such groups in the future.

A warning about what such Islamist groups are actually doing—even as they exploit opportunities afforded them by law enforcement and government agencies seeking authentic "community partnerships"—comes from Dr. Zuhdi Jasser of the American Islamic Forum for Democracy and the American Islamic Leadership Coalition. In March 2011, he testified before the House Homeland Security Committee (http://tinyurl.com/4es8aa2):

> When we speak about "cooperation of Muslims with law enforcement," what is more important is the growing culture of driving Muslims away from cooperation, partnership, and identity with our nation and its security forces. Our civil rights should be protected and defended, but the predominant message to our communities should be attachment, defense, and identification with America, not alienation and separation.

Too many so-called Muslim leadership groups in America, Like the Council on American Islamic Relations (CAIR) or Muslim Advocates, have specifically told Muslims across the nation, for example, not to speak to the FBI or law enforcement unless they are accompanied by an attorney. Rather than thanking the FBI for ferreting out radicals within our community, they have criticized sting operations as being "entrapment" - a claim that has not stood the test of anti-terrorism court cases since 9/11. Informants end up being showcased as bad apples and subjects of lawsuits rather than patriots. While individual rights must always be protected, operations like the FBI conducted in December 2010 in Portland, Oregon are commonplace in other types of cases such as drug enforcement and racketeering cases. So, why would they not be acceptable in terror cases?

[34] Investigative reporter and author of *Infiltration: How Muslim Spies and Subversives have Penetrated* Washington Paul Sperry addressed the question of whether it is "guilt by association" to tie Suhail Khan to the Muslim Brotherhood:

> Suhail Khan, a major Republican supporter of the Ground Zero mosque, has been lobbying GOP leaders on the Hill to back off their opposition. He's got their ear, mainly because he portrays himself as a moderate, patriotic Muslim. Yet newly surfaced videos contradict that.
>
> Khan, a Bush administration vet who sits on the board of the American Conservative Union, assures skeptics that "Park 51 community center" imam Feisal Rauf is a "moderate." Fears over the mosque are overblown, he insists, fomented by "anti-Muslim bigotry." In a recent letter to fellow Republicans, he warned the party was "alienating millions of Arab-American and Muslim-American voters."
>
> But Khan's assurances ring hollow against his own connections to radicals. While he strenuously denies such ties, evidence has emerged—including exclusive video footage—that exposes Khan comfortably in the company of known Islamic extremists.

* * *

Khan may plead "guilt by association"—but he's done a lot of associating with a lot of guilty people and groups over the years. At a bare minimum, he's completely failed at identifying the bad guys—contrary to the record of those he brands as "anti-Muslim bigots."

Republicans, beware.

[35] David Horowitz first warned of the threat posed to the conservative movement, the Republican Party and the country by Grover Norquist, Suhail Khan and their Muslim Brotherhood associates in a signed introduction to the 12,000-word article by Frank Gaffney that *Front Page Magazine* published in December 2003 In it, he called the article "the most disturbing that we at FrontPageMag.com have ever published." Among the highlights of the introduction were the following observations (http://tinyurl.com/29glebo):

> It is with a heavy heart… that I am posting this article, which is the most complete documentation extant of Grover Norquist's activities in behalf of the Islamist Fifth Column. I have confronted Grover about these issues and have talked to others who have done likewise. But it has been left to Frank Gaffney and a few others, including Daniel Pipes and Steven Emerson, to make the case and to suffer the inevitable re-criminations that have followed earlier disclosures of some aspects of this story.
>
> Up to now, the controversy over these charges has been dismissed or swept under the rug, as a clash of personalities or the product of one of those intra-bureaucratic feuds so familiar to the Washington scene. Unfortunately, this is wishful thinking. The reality is much more serious. No one reading this document to its bitter end will confuse its claims and confirming evidence with those of a political cat fight.
>
> On the basis of the evidence assembled here, it seems beyond dispute that Grover Norquist has formed alliances with prominent Islamic radicals who have ties to the Saudis and to Libya and to Palestine Islamic Jihad, and who are now under indictment by U.S. authorities. Equally troubling is that the arrests of these individuals and their exposure as agents of terrorism have not resulted in noticeable second thoughts on Grover's part or any meaningful effort to dissociate himself from his unsavory friends.
>
> * * *
>
> Together they gained access to the White House for Alamoudi and Sami al-Arian and others with similar agendas who used their cachet to spread Islamist influence to the American military and the prison system and the universities and the political arena with untold consequences for the nation.
>
> Many have been reluctant to support these charges or to make them public because they involve a prominent conservative. I am familiar with these attitudes from my years on the Left. Loyalty is an important political value, but there comes a point where loyalty to friends or to

parties comes into conflict with loyalty to fundamental principles and ultimately to one's country. Grover's activities have reached that point. E.M. Forster, a weak-spirited liberal, once said that if he had to choose between betraying his country and his friends, he "hoped [he] would have the guts" to betray his country.

[36] On Sean Hannity's radio program on February 15, 2011, Khan qualified his statement by saying, "If there is a Muslim Brotherhood, I'm not aware of it. You know, to my knowledge, there is no official presence of the Muslim Brotherhood in this country" (http://tinyurl.com/p6cb52f).

[37] Testifying before the House Judiciary Committee on May 23, 2000 in opposition to the Secret Evidence Repeal Act (which they identified as H.R 2121, four prominent Jewish organizations known for championing civil liberties—the Anti-Defamation League, the American Jewish Congress, B'nai B'rith International, Hadassah and the Jewish Council for Public Affairs—explained their concerns about the proposed legislation (http://tinyurl.com/qdzksmd). Particularly relevant were two of their conclusions:

> *H.R. 2121 Unduly Restricts the Ability of Government Officials to Protect Essential Confidential Sources and Methods.*
>
> Senior law enforcement authorities in the U.S. have testified on numerous occasions before Congress that terrorist organizations seek to use the United States to plan, organize, and raise funds for terrorist activities here and abroad. H.R. 2121 too-broadly restricts the ability of law enforcement officials to protect intelligence sources. In some instances, because the information provided by intelligence sources is so singular in nature, known only by very few individuals, revealing it to suspected terrorists detained in this country would compromise those sources—who may risk death if exposed.
>
> *H.R. 2121 Could Force the Government to Release Terrorists Who Threaten National Security.*
>
> Because this legislation forces the government to choose between releasing a suspect or exposing intelligence sources, H.R. 2121 could lead to the release of individuals currently being detained who do, in fact, pose a terrorist threat. Law enforcement officials maintain that they cannot and will not expose sources and threaten the lives of personnel in order to move forward with a prosecution. Forcing this choice is tantamount to the ensuring the release of these suspects.

[38] Sami al-Arian's campaign to repeal the secret evidence statute was the subject of a lengthy and sympathetic July 28, 2002 *Washington Post* article entitled, "Talking Out of School. Was an Islamic Professor Exercising His Freedom or Promoting Terror?" by Richard Leiby (http://tinyurl.com/q7a3v2t).

[39] Presumably, this is the meeting with Suhail Khan referred to by Abdurahman Alamoudi in his June 2001 introduction of the then-White House full-time volunteer (http://tinyurl.com/o9kpo7v). Cited remarks begin at 1:05.

[40] In Suhail Khan's debate with Cleta Mitchell, David Horowitz and Frank Gaffney on Sean Hannity's radio program on February 15, 2011, he declared:

> I'm a conservative activist who focuses on conservative issues. If there is a Muslim Brotherhood, I'm not aware of it. You know, to my knowledge, there is no official presence of the Muslim Brotherhood in this country. But that's up to debate. I'll let the experts on the Muslim Brotherhood discuss that. All I know is I'm not part of it. That's, you know, I'm part of ACU. I'm a Reagan conservative who wants to cut taxes and preserve life and have a strong defense. That's what I work on day in and day out. And one of my other projects is religious freedom, promoting religious freedom for all Christians, Jews, and Muslims around the country and around the globe.

Suhail Khan's involvement with "interfaith dialogue" coincides with a priority accorded such activities by the Muslim Brotherhood. In fact, Khan works closely with the president of the largest Brotherhood front, the Islamic Society of North America, Mohamed Magid, and other prominent Brothers to promote "bridge-building" with other faiths. (At JihadWatch.org, Islam expert and best-selling author Robert Spencer helps clarify the Muslim Brotherhood's true purpose in building bridges with non-Muslims by citing its chief ideologue, Sayyid Qutb: "The chasm between Islam and Jahiliyyah [the society of unbelievers] is great, and a bridge is not to be built across it so that the people on the two sides may mix with each other, but only so that the people of Jahiliyyah may come over to Islam" (http://tinyurl.com/o8vgmv8).

For example, Khan tried to call attention during his February 15th Hannity debate to a trip he had organized to Auschwitz in August 2010 for Imams Magid and Sidiqqi and other Islamists together with non-Muslim official and religious Americans. (For a sense of the influence operations use to which such exercises are put, see a September 27, 2010 press release by the Konrad Adenauer Foundation entitled "US Imams and Muslim leaders Make Historic Trip to Auschwitz" (http://tinyurl.com/pydfvmy). Khan and Magid teamed up to make a similar excursion to Auschwitz in May 2013 (see the May 28, 2013 ISNA press release entitled "Global Muslim Delegation Issues Unprecedented Statement Against Anti-Semitism" (http://tinyurl.com/nshonur).

[41] Suhail Khan was a signer of an August 17, 2010 open letter placed with the *New York Times* blog ("Muslim and Arab Republicans Take Issue With G.O.P. on Mosque," by Bernie Becker, http://tinyurl.com/qzzxkag) together with five other Muslims who described themselves as "loyal Americans who are active members of the Republican Party."

The signatories rebuked others in the GOP for opposing the so-called "Cordoba House" then proposed for a site near the destroyed World Trade Center, declaring, "We cannot support victory at the expense of the U.S. Constitution or the Arab and Muslim community in America." Several of the other signers had ties to Grover Norquist including (now-Virginia Delegate) David Ramadan (see, "Grover Norquist's New Muslim Protégé," by Kenneth Timmerman, *Front Page Magazine*, September 26, 2011 and Norquist's wife, Samah (http://tinyurl.com/ogmcaxo).

Middle East expert and author Daniel Pipes described Mrs. Norquist's background in an April 14, 2005 essay (subsequently updated on June 21, 2011) entitled "Is Grover Norquist an Islamist?" (http://tinyurl.com/yzqmtf6). Highlights included:

> Norquist married Samah Alrayyes, a Palestinian Muslim, on November 27, 2004. On the one hand, Islamic law limits a Muslim woman to marrying a man who is Muslim; this is not an abstract dictum but a very serious imperative, with many "honor" killings having resulted from a woman ignoring her family's wishes. On the other hand, they were married in a church by the Rev. Stephen T. Melius of Weston United Methodist Church in Weston, Massachusetts.

> Alrayyes (now known as Samah Alrayyes Norquist) has radical Islamic credentials of her own; she served as communications director at the Islamic Free Market Institute, the Islamist organization Norquist helped found. Now, she is employed as a public affairs officer at the U.S. Agency for International Development—and so it appears that yet another Islamist finds employment in a branch of the U.S. government.

In an September 30, 2005 update, Dr. Pipes quotes from a biography of Samah Alrayyes Norquist's when she worked at USAID (http://tinyurl.com/p6wv8eo):

> [Samah Norquist is] the Public Affairs Specialist for Arab and Muslim outreach at the Bureau of Legislative and Public affairs at USAID. In her position, she works on developing and implementing communications and public affairs planning with regard to various Muslim and Arab outreach issues including USAID activities in Iraq, Afghanistan, Middle and Near East and many parts of the Muslim world where AID is present. This includes serving as a liaison with Muslim and Arab American interest groups to brief them on USAID activities in the developing world and coordination of the Agency's participation in events, conferences, and discussions designed to educate the publics

about American foreign assistance. In addition, Norquist attends inter-agency meetings representing USAID on issues related to Arab and Muslim outreach and public diplomacy.

Then, in a June 11, 2011 update, Dr. Pipes cites "The Norquist Cell: Operation GroverKhan," published on that day by Gary Johnson at *Family Security Matters* (http://tinyurl.com/puuhcxq) and his two conclusions: "First, Grover Norquist is an ad-vocate for legitimating Shariah Compliant Finance as an ethical alternative to capitalism. And second, Norquist's chosen battle ground for this subversive effort has been and re-mains the chiefly influence- and lobby-based contracts drawn up through USAID."

[42] This photograph subsequently became a political liability for President Bush. Sev-eral examples of the criticism to which he was subjected were collected at Democrats.com (http://tinyurl.com/lesrdeb).

[43] The transactional nature of this statement and Grover Norquist's central role in its realization is evident from the following account in the *Wall Street Journal* article entitled "In Difficult Times, Muslims Count On Unlikely Advocate; Norquist, Famed Tax Foe, Offers Washington Access, Draws Flak": "Twice during the debate, Mr. Norquist says, Mr. Rove phoned him at home to draw his attention to the remark and urge him to 'put the word out' among Muslims." The *Journal* adds, however, that, "Mr. Rove says he doesn't remember making such calls" (http://tinyurl.com/oewwess).

The role played by Norquist and others at the Islamic Free Market Institute was made a part of the Congressional Record by Rep. Frank Wolf (R-VA) in a speech deliv-ered on the floor of the House of Representatives on October 4, 2011. He said, in part:

> Mr. Norquist himself served as a key facilitator between Al-Arian, Alamoudi and the White House, according to Mary Jacoby's reporting in March 2003 in *The St. Petersburg Times*. She reported that "In June 2001, Al-Arian was among the members of the American Muslim Council invited to the White House complex...."

[44] Sami al-Arian's wife, Nahla, also joined the family effort to eliminate the counter-terrorism tool they called "secret evidence" by testifying in favor of the "Secret Evidence Repeal Act." In an appearance before the House Judiciary Committee on May 23, 2000 Mrs. al-Arian painted a touching picture of her brother, Dr. Mazen al-Najjar, then being held awaiting deportation on the basis of secret evidence (http://tinyurl.com/o4e67lx). In the end, al-Najjar was deported n 2002 for his leadership role in the Palestinian Islamic Jihad which Stephen Emerson's Investigative Project on Terrorism notes involved service "on the PIJ Majlis Shura, or the terrorist group's governing board" (http://tinyurl.com/3pcfmz6).

[45] A December 2001 posting on the website of Americans United for the Separation fo Chuch and State (White House Hires Muslim-Outreach Staffer reprised a report by a PBS television program that made it sound as though Khan had actually been given a *paid* position in the White House (http://tinyurl.com/p65waka):

> The Bush administration has hired a Muslim to work in the White House Office of Public Liaison and foster better interaction between the government and American Muslims.
>
> Suhail Khan, who had previously served on the staff of former Rep. Tom Campbell (R-Calif.), will assist other administration officials in attempting to improve Muslim relations and will help promote better understanding between Muslims, Christians and Jews.
>
> As first reported by "Religion and Ethics NewsWeekly," a PBS television program, Muslim leaders expressed pleasure with Khan's new position in the administration but pointed out that there are still no Muslims in decision-making positions in the federal government.
>
> The Bush administration has made repeated overtures to the Muslim community, a pattern started by the president during the 2000 campaign.

[46] In the course of the Khan-Horowitz debate on the Hannity program on February 14, 2011 (http://tinyurl.com/ox5t4ex), reference was made to a White House access list of dozens of Islamist operatives. While the cross talk made the exact content of the debaters' remarks difficult to follow, Khan seemed to acknowledge its authenticity, while denying that his name was on top of it. In fact, as *Insight Magazine* reported Grover Norquist's name was at the top. (http://tinyurl.com/8v2dvr)

> A White House memo obtained by Insight prepared for coordinating Muslim and Arab-American "public-liaison" events with the White House shows that the Islamic Institute was instrumental in establishing the connection. The memo, from early 2001, provides lists of invitees and the name, date of birth and Social Security number of each. Norquist, as the first chairman of the Islamic Institute, tops the list.

[47] For more on the now-defunct National Coalition to Protect Political Freedoms, see: http://tinyurl.com/pg2xpgo

[48] Paul Sperry, *Infiltration: How Muslim Spies and Subversives have Penetrated Washington*, p. 281. (http://tinyurl.com/qzz9r73)

[49] The Council on American Islamic Relations was listed as an unindicted co-conspirator in U.S. v Holy Land Foundation *et.al.* as a member of the Muslim Brotherhood's U.S. Palestine Committee and as a member of Hamas in the United States (http://tinyurl.com/3uhx6lh and http://tinyurl.com/q8n69co). The connections between CAIR, the Brotherhood's U.S. Palestine Committee and Hamas was also attested to by Assistant Attorney General Ronald Weich in a February 12, 2010 letter to Congresswoman Sue Myrick (http://tinyurl.com/o977rcm).

[50] One of those not invited to attend the Muslim outreach meetings was Dr. Zuhdi Jasser. Insofar as the Muslim Brotherhood was in a position to dominate the government's interactions with the Muslim American community, its hostility towards pro-American, anti-Islamist yet devout Muslims like Jasser ensure that they would be excluded. It is an incalculable tragedy that, as a result of the success of the Brotherhood influence operation enabled by Grover Norquist and Suhail Khan that President Bush did not have a chance to hear in the hours after 9/11 the sort of statement Dr. Jasser made to the House Homeland Security Committee on March 10, 2011:

> As we have watched the long overdue changes in the Middle East, at long last the threat that the Muslim Brotherhood poses to security around the world has been brought to the forefront. The Brotherhood is the leading Islamist organization in the world. It has also over the past century hatched many of the most violent Islamist organizations in the world. We have not transitioned this newly understood concern to the operations of the Brotherhood and like-minded organizations and leaders within the United States. Our domestic and foreign policy should be the same on this issue.

[51] Muzammil Sidiqqi has endorsed the quintessential character of civilization jihad: a tactical approach known as "gradualism." As Ryan Mauro reported in "Nothing Moderate About ISNA's Conference Line-Up" (http://tinyurl.com/q3g749b) about the 2013 Islamic Society of North America annual conference at which its past president, Sidiqqi, was a featured speaker:

> In 1996, [Sidiqqi] advocated the Islamist doctrine of gradualism, saying that Muslims "should participate in the [democratic] system to safeguard our interest and try to bring gradual change for the right cause....We must not forget that Allah's rules have to be established in all lands, and all our efforts should lead to that direction."
>
> In 2001, Siddiqi explained that he hoped that *sharia* Law, including its criminal justice system, would come to America. He said, "The criminal of the *sharia* is not practiced here and it is not even required for Muslims to practice the criminal law in a non-Islamic state...Once

more people accept Islam, *insha'allah*, this will lead to the implementation of sharia in all areas."

As Mauro has previously reported ("The Islamists' Multi-Staged Strategy for Victory Over the West," January 21, 2013), Sidiqqi is not alone in espousing gradualism (http://tinyurl.com/p27b84j).

> "Gradualism in applying the *sharia* is a wise requirement to follow," [Yousef al-] Qaradawi declared, stating that Mohammed followed it.
>
> The Islamists, especially the Muslim Brotherhood, have always worked in stages. In December [2012], the Brotherhood's Supreme Guide, Mohamed Badi, outlined six phases:
>
> (1) *Sharia* over the individual; (2) *Sharia* over the family; (3) *Sharia* over the society; (4) *Sharia* over the government; (5) Resurrection of the Caliphate and finally, (6) "Mastership of the world."

[52] American Conservative Union Board Member Cleta Mitchell told Sean Hannity on his program on February 15, 2003: "[Suhail Khan] worked in the Bush White House. He had a security clearance from the Bush White House and the United States government and it's hard for me to fathom, frankly, that Suhail would be an operative of Muslim extremists working in the White House with a security clearance" (http://tinyurl.com/p6cb52f). Cited remarks begin at 11:18.

Recent events involving vast and highly destructive breaches of security by individuals who should never have obtained clearances have called public attention to a problem that national security professionals have been aware of for many years: The process whereby background investigations are conducted and security clearances issued is broken.

In fact, according to a front-page article in the New *York Times* ("Security Check Firm Said to Have Defrauded U.S.") on January 23, 2013, the Department of Justice has joined a whistleblower's civil lawsuit against United States Investigative Services (USIS), a firm that began doing background checks for security clearances when the Clinton administration privatized some of that work *in 1996* (http://tinyurl.com/ogju5xe). According to the *Times* over 650,000 such investigations were improperly approved thanks to a process the firm called "flushing" or "dumping": "Government lawyers accused the company of releasing investigations that had not been complete, a practice referred to in court documents as 'dumping.' The government quoted from internal company emails to argue that the practice was widespread."

Matters have reached such a pass that, on October 30, 2013, a bipartisan group of U.S. senators introduced legislation meant to address that reality. Two of the sponsors described the problem this way: Sen. Clare McCaskill (D-MO) said, "There are systemic failures in the current process that are jeopardizing our ability to protect our nation's secrets and our secure facilities."

Sen. Kelly Ayotte (R-ME) added: "There are serious gaps in the government's security clearance system, and our bipartisan legislation will help close those gaps by putting in place safeguards to better identify potential risks. We must ensure that individuals who hold security clearances are qualified, fit to serve, and don't pose a danger to the workforce or our national security" (http://tinyurl.com/nm6rfgv).

[53] Interestingly, this phrase was repeated virtually verbatim in a memorandum American Conservative Union Board member (and chairwoman of the American Conservative Union Foundation) Cleta Mitchell wrote her fellow directors on September 21, 2011. It was used to dissuade the ACU leadership from addressing further the persistent questions about Grover Norquist and Suhail Khan's Islamist ties and activities. A copy of the memo was leaked on February 12, 2012 to the George Soros-funded leftist blog, ThinkProgress (http://tinyurl.com/pxspfwf). Based on Ms. Mitchell's representations, the ACU Board adopted a resolution endorsing Norquist and Khan and effectively repudiating Frank Gaffney for making "false and unfounded" charges against them (http://tinyurl.com/ppwy4z3).

[54] David Keene authored an op-ed column in *The Hill*, in which he explained why anti-Islamist Muslims were not more in evidence: "The problem is that moderate Muslims control few organizations and have virtually no voice. Most of them, in fact, know better than to challenge the Wahhabis." (Cited in "Friends in High Places," by Mary Jacoby *St. Petersburg Times*, March 11, 2003 (http://tinyurl.com/nohsvmr).

[55] In addition to ad hominem charges of "racism" and "bigotry" and expulsion of those accused of it from conservative movement meetings, Norquist reportedly also invoked President Bush, Karl Rove and the White House to enlist allies in his efforts to silence critics. As Byron York reported:

> Heightening the tension was Norquist's angry assertion that the White House, and in particular chief political adviser Karl Rove, supported his racism-and-bigotry argument. One witness quotes Norquist as saying, "This is terrible. Karl's upset because we're insulting the people who helped Bush win the election." Another witness recalls that Norquist "said the president and Rove were angry at the conference." In addition, Norquist sent an e-mail to American Conservative Union board members saying that "[t]he White House and the press are increasingly angry with [the American Conservative Union] for some indefensible statements and actions at CPAC this year."

Interestingly, York adds that, "In a recent interview, Norquist denied using the White House to support his accusations: 'I never invoke the president or Karl Rove on this position—in anything.'" (http://tinyurl.com/nvr4emj)

AFTERWORD

On February 5, 2014, the Departments of State and Homeland Security published an announcement in the Federal Register that effectively cleared the way for individuals who had engaged in "limited" material support for terrorism to apply for asylum in the United States. On the face of it, this is a lunatic idea.

That is especially true at a time when a crackdown on the Muslim Brotherhood in Egypt and elsewhere in the Middle East is creating a demand for safe havens on the part of the organization's operatives who, according to the Brotherhood's own documents, seek "to destroy Western civilization from within... by their hands [meaning, those of Americans and other Western peoples]."

The question occurs: Why would the Obama administration want to make it easier to have material supporters of terrorism gain entry to this country? Unfortunately, as the online course entitled "The Muslim Brotherhood in America" (MuslimBrotherhoodinAmerica.com) makes clear, this is hardly the only—and certainly not the first—instance of such an accommodation to Islamists that has been made by Team Obama. Other examples include:

* efforts to circumscribe First Amendment rights so as to prevent "offense" to Muslims;

* implementing rules of engagement for U.S. personnel in combat theaters designed to do the same;

* purging training materials used by the FBI, the military, the intelligence community and the Department of Homeland Security that Muslims might find objectionable;

* requiring that, before training of such agencies' personnel about "countering violent extremism" can be conducted in the future, consultations must be held with "community partners" (read, Muslim organizations usually associated with the Brotherhood) to ensure that the trainers and their proposed materials are acceptable to such partners; and

* defining as "workplace violence" Maj. Nidal Hassan's jihadist attack at Ft. Hood.

Troubling as these previous acts of submission to the Islamists' demands may be, the Obama administration's decision to refuse to enforce fully the nation's material support for terrorism laws is arguably even more alarming. It will, after all, not only result in more jihadists coming here. In all likelihood, it will also give additional latitude to those already here who believe that their Islamic doctrine of shariah obliges them to provide charitable contributions (or zakat) to those waging jihad.

Easing, if not actually eliminating outright, such legal restrictions has been a declared goal of President Obama since June 4, 2009 when, in his first Muslim outreach speech in Cairo entitled "New Beginnings," he announced that:

> Freedom of religion is central to the ability of peoples to live together. We must always examine the ways in which we protect it. For instance, in the United States, rules on charitable giving have made it harder for Muslims to fulfill their religious obligation. That's why I'm committed to working with American Muslims to ensure that they can fulfill zakat.

Of course, as former federal prosecutor Andrew C. McCarthy has observed,

> There are, in fact, no American laws or rules that make it harder for Muslims to give to charity. What we have are laws against material support of terrorism—against using devices like charitable fronts to channel money to jihadists. Those laws are not directed at Muslims. They apply to everyone but are applied most often to Muslims, because Muslims carry out most anti-American terrorism. (http://tinyurl.com/3b6nw9m)

Consequently, dismantling such laws has been a priority for prominent American Islamists, including two who feature in the Norquist Dossier: former Islamic Free Market Institute chairman and George W. Bush administration official Suhail Khan and Mohamed Magid, the president of the Muslim Brotherhood's Islamic Society of North America.

For example, as noted in Part 4 of "The Muslim Brotherhood in America," Khan has forged with leftists a red-green axis operating under the banner of the Charity and Security Network to promote the notion that respect for religious freedom requires the government to allow Muslims to make zakat payments to organizations of their choice—to include Muslim Brotherhood and other Islamist ones. The Network's stated mission is "to eliminate barriers counterterrorism measures create for legitimate charitable development, human rights and conflict- resolution work." (Emphasis added.)

What is "legitimate" for shariah-promoting Muslims like Mohamed Magid and Suhail Khan, however, is not hard to discern. Zakat in all its forms, like the rest of shariah, is perfect, divinely directed and immutable. By definition, it is legitimate. And the notion that some man-made laws could make it otherwise is inconceivable, unacceptable and an offensive provocation.

In furtherance of this objective, the Network website featured on November 25, 2008 a post that declared, among other things:

> Donors are growing increasingly weary as court decisions against chari-
> ties have created an environment of suspicion for numerous Muslim
> charities. The decrease in contributions will lead to smaller numbers of
> people receiving relief.

> Verdicts such as the one delivered in the Holy Land Foundation trial
> have caused many Muslim charities to suffer decreases in charitable giv-
> ing. Since September 11, 2001, several Muslim charities have been
> shutdown by the government for having connections to Middle Eastern
> countries.

"Either you risk having your group shut down, your funds frozen and your leaders prosecuted by providing aid in international hot spots where people are neediest,
or you stay away to stay safe," said Kay Guinane, Program Manager of the Charity
and Security Network. "Neither choice is acceptable for a society that prides itself on
its respect for human life," she added.

The bottom line for Khan's Charity and Security Network is:

> Looking forward, there is an urgent need for the government to reex-
> amine policies that target the nonprofit sector with little prospect of
> stopping terrorism and at the expense of important humanitarian and
> human rights work and the constitutional rights of U.S. donors and
> U.S.-based charities.

Magid shares this sentiment. In June 2009, National Public Radio reported that:

> Imam Magid... thinks the government should take another look at the
> rules [regarding material support for terrorism] that were set up eight
> years ago – which is why he was thrilled when he heard President
> Obama tell Muslims that he understood the rules hinder their religious
> freedom.

> "Oh, I clapped actually!" he says, laughing. "I said, 'Yes! Finally some-
> body is mentioning it publicly!' And coming from the president him-
> self, that means a lot."

> Now, Magid says, the president needs to turn his words into policies –
> and do it before Ramadan begins in August [2009].
> (http://tinyurl.com/llktwn)

Messrs. Magid and Khan have also partnered in an initiative called Muflehun
("successful" in Arabic), a reference to a Koranic passage (3:104) that superficially

appears benign ("promoting good works and justice"). But to the shariah-adherent, *muflehun* is a clear call to achieve dominance by coopting the infidel.

Muflehun's website describes its mission as: "To help establish a community that promotes good works and justice while peaceably working against injustice and wrongs" (http://tinyurl.com/lzwlrps).

As this book reminds us, the Muslim Brotherhood believes that the imposition of shariah and the reestablishment of an Islamist government, the Caliphate, to rule according to it are the ultimate "good works." They are also necessary preconditions for "justice." The Brotherhood wages civilization jihad to "work against" those things—notably the Constitution of the United States and the freedoms it guarantees—that impede the realization of its goals.

Subsequent to the publication of the first edition of this book, a very comprehensive narrative of the events it describes was published at The Clarion Project by Ryan Mauro, a brilliant investigative reporter and expert on Islamism. It complements and affirms the evidence presented in the Statement of Facts.

It behooves true conservatives, Republicans and, indeed, the American people as a whole to resist such subversive operations and to expose and counter those who enable them.

Frank J. Gaffney, Jr.
President and CEO
Center for Security Policy
March 28, 2014

APPENDIX I

Letter to Former Attorney General Michael Mukasey from Cleta Mitchell

March 21, 2014

Hand-Delivered Personally
The Honorable Michael B. Mukasey
81 51 Attorney General of the United States

Re: Response to your letter to Cleta Mitchell

Dear General Mukasey:

Enclosed is the letter you wrote to me a few weeks ago.

I was rather startled and surprised to receive this letter from you - you are a senior and internationally recognized expert in the field of law enforcement and national security and I have absolutely no involvement or expertise in that field.

It was and continues to be mystifying to me that you would join with a group of experts in the area of national security, muster all the firepower represented by those with whom you signed the letter and train your vast capability on issues regarding our country's role in the world on ... me.

Someone who has absolutely nothing to do with national security in any way, shape or form. And that the greatest threat you and your colleagues can identify with regard to the nation's security is the composition of the board of directors of the American Conservative Union.

You, and the others who signed the letter to me look, in my estimation, quite ridiculous. That view is shared by everyone with whom I have discussed this bizarre situation.

Apparently, one of two things happened to result in your sending me the letter enclosed in this envelope: either the terrorist threat is completely over and you and your colleagues are casting about for something else to work on (like sending letters to people wholly removed from the field of national security), or Frank Gaffney has duped you.

To be clear about who I am and what I do: I am an election and campaign finance attorney with roles in various conservative organizations. I know absolutely nothing about national security other than what I hear and read in the news.

Why, pray tell, do you CARE who serves on the ACU board of directors? Is that seriously a concern of yours or a threat to national security?

Does it strike you as at all strange that Frank Gaffney is obsessed with CPAC, ACU, Grover Norquist, Suhail Kahn and apparently, now, Cleta Mitchell? A better use of your time and influence might have been to urge Frank to work on something useful and to stop his ceaseless tirades on these topics.

You and I have never met personally. However, in my role as a campaign finance and election law attorney, I was essentially "smuggled" into a meeting you hosted in the fall of 2008 when you were Attorney General of the United States. The meeting was hosted by you at the Dept of Justice. I was invited by one of the very few attorneys at DOJ who thought there should be at least SOME representation of conservative groups at a meeting that had been called by the leftist leadership of the Voting Section (something you did nothing to change when you were attorney general) and to which no conservatives had been invited. I was allowed to attend in my capacity as Chairman of the American Conservative Union. There was exactly ONE other conservative organization present at the meeting at which you presided. There were at least 40 leftist groups present.

The subject and purpose of the meeting was to underscore DOJ's "promise" that the full efforts of the DOJ would be dedicated to ensure the protection of the voting rights in the 2008 election. But where were the voter integrity groups - who should have comprised half of the audience? Groups concerned about and committed to integrity of the elections? Where was the commitment of the DOJ under your command to ensuring compliance with the election laws of America?

I was appalled by what I witnessed. These are the very organizations and individuals who fight everything the Republican National Lawyers Association does and stands for.

I do have expertise on the subject of the election laws of our country and ensuring that elections are honest and comply with the laws. And my only experience with you on ANY subject prior to receipt of the letter you sent me last month was observing your role in supporting the politically correct leftists who hate all that conservatives believe regarding adhering to the rule of law governing our elections.

If you have something to say to me, I'm really not hard to find. I can be reached at (xxx) xxx-xxxx (office), my cell (xxx) xxx-xxxx or email: cmitchell@foley.com. You can call me or email me any time. You don't need to sign some ridiculous letter directed at the internal decisions of some conservative organization.

And I hope you will actually focus your attention, your reputation, expertise and skills on real national security issues and be wary of those who use and abuse your good name for their own selfish purposes.

Sincerely,
Cleta Mitchell, Esq.

APPENDIX II

Letter To Cleta Mitchell From Former Attorney General Michael Mukasey

April 18, 2014

Cleta Mitchell, Esq.
Foley & Lardner LLP
3000 K Street, N.W.
Suite 600
Washington, D.C. 20007-5109

Dear Ms. Mitchell:

This is in response to your letter of March 21, 2014, which you thrust into my hands (or "HAND DELIVERED PERSONALLY" as the envelope proclaims) at a reception in Washington sponsored by the Republican National Lawyers Association.

Your letter seems to make three general points:

1) Because, as you would have it, my principal credential relates to national security, and because the question of who serves on the board of the American Conservative Union does not implicate issues of national security, that question is none of my business.

2) That I involved myself in something that is none of my business (because it does not implicate matters of national security) means I must have been beguiled into doing so by Frank Gaffney, who is "obsessed" with things and people that are none of his business, either.

3) My own conservative bona fides is tainted by having presided as Attorney General at a meeting at the Justice Department at which "only ONE other conservative organization was present"—a meeting attended by "at least 40 leftist groups" whose "subject and purpose ... was to underscore DOJ's 'promise' that the full efforts of the DOJ would be dedicated to ensure the protection of the voting rights [sic] in the 2008 election," a meeting at which you detected no concern for the integrity of the voting process.

Taking your last point first, I recall only one meeting at the Justice Department attended by outside groups that was in fact set up by the person who was in charge of outreach in my office, and who dealt with the groups themselves; they were clamoring for the meeting. My recollection is that it took place in the conference room of the Attorney General's office—which I don't think would comfortably seat representatives of 40 groups, although I take "40" in your letter to be a figure of speech meaning "a lot." I recall hearing out various people, making the point that we would protect voting rights—as we did—and sending the participants on their merry way. If, as you say, you are an expert on election law, you know that voter eligibility even in federal elections is a matter of state law, and you are no doubt aware that the Justice Department during my tenure supported strongly the use by states of photo identification requirements, and the right of states to purge their voter rolls of names of those no longer qualified to vote (often by reason of being dead).

Going back to your second point, be assured that I did my own reading before arriving at my views, and I do not consider myself to have been beguiled by Frank Gaffney or anyone else. Actually, I think any open-minded person—let alone one knowledgeable about (or at least concerned with) national security—would be troubled by the evidence laid out in the Statement of Facts that accompanied the letter ten of us sent you on February 11, 2014. I note that you do not address any of that evidence.

As to your first point, I think that the infiltration of organizations by people committed to the destruction of this country, and their sympathizers, is a proper focus for someone concerned with national security—a subject about which you concede complete ignorance. If there are people who call themselves conservatives and who profess concern with protecting this country and its values, but who associate with and support people who are trying to undermine everything this country stands for, I think it is perfectly proper to point that out. As a primer on this subject, I recommend a book called "The Grand Jihad" by Andrew McCarthy, who also signed the letter that so offended you. For your convenience, I have sent you with this letter a copy of that book. Please read it and share it with your friends.

I very much hope that the American Conservative Union will address, as you have not—either in your September 2011 memorandum to its board or in your most recent letter to me—the evidence of such infiltration in its ranks.

Very truly yours,
Michael B. Mukasey

Made in the USA
Lexington, KY
03 October 2014